An Atlas of
Maritime Florida

Roger C. Smith, James J. Miller,
Sean M. Kelley, Linda G. Harbin

Florida Bureau of Archaeological Research
Division of Historical Resources

University Press of Florida

Gainesville/Tallahassee/Tampa/Boca Raton
Pensacola/Orlando/Miami/Jacksonville

01 00 99 98 97 96 6 5 4 3 2 1

Library of Congress Cataloging-in-Publication Data

An atlas of maritime Florida / Roger C. Smith . . . [et al.]
p. cm.
Includes bibliographical references.
Contents: Physical environment—Growth of maritime Florida—Maritime industries—Navigation and ship types—Hazards and aids to navigation—Ship losses and shipwrecks.
ISBN 0-8130-1512-X
1. Navigation—History—Florida—Maps. 2. Discoveries in geography—Maps. 3. Shipwrecks—Florida—Maps. I. Smith, Roger C. 1949– . II. Florida. Dept. of State. III. Florida Bureau of Archaeological Research. IV. Florida. Division of Historical Resources.
G1316.P5 A8   1997 <G&M>
623.89'229759—DC20

96-35130
CIP
MAPS

Financial support for this project was provided by Florida Department of Community Affairs, Coastal Management Program, using funds made available through the National Oceanic and Atmospheric Administrationunder the Coastal Zone Management Act of 1972, as amended.

FLORIDA
HERITAGE

Florida Department of State
Sandra B. Mortham, Secretary of State

Acknowledgments

We gratefully acknowledge the financial support of the Coastal Management Program, National Oceanic and Atmospheric Administration, administered in Florida by the Department of Community Affairs. The assistance and cooperation of Ralph Cantral and the program staff are most appreciated. We were efficiently and graciously assisted by Joan Morris, supervisor of the Florida Photographic Archives, who guided us in the selection of historical photographs. Robert Bell, supervisor of the Department of State Graphics Office, freely provided advice, assistance, supplies, and use of equipment, without which our task would have been more expensive and difficult. We thank Dixie Nims, Florida Department of Commerce, Division of Tourism, for selecting and supplying modern photographs, and Dr. Barbara Purdy, University of Florida, Department of Anthropology, for data on the distribution of prehistoric canoes. We appreciate the generosity and patience of Paul Rutkovsky, who allowed us the use of his printer for proof production. Staff of the Bureau of Archaeological Research, especially Hope Kurtz, assisted in many ways with administrative support, information gathering, review of various drafts, and proof reading.

Picture Credits

Cover design and illustration by Synergy Design group. Florida Photo Archives: pp. iv, 1, 2, 10, 12, 14, 16 top, 17, 18, 19 top, 20, 21, 22, 24 top, 30, 32, 35, and 36. **Lorant, Stephen, ed., 1965,** *The New World*, **Duell, Sloan and Pearce, New York:** pp. 6 and 8 after deBry, **Theodore, 1591,** *Great and Small Voyages, Florida volume. Harpers Magazine*, **1911, July (p. 275):** p. 16 bottom. **Florida Department of Commerce, Robert Overton, photographer.** p. 19 bottom. **Randier, Jean, 1980,** *Marine Navigational Instruments*, **J. Murray, London:** pp. 24 bottom, and 25 top and middle. **Si-Tex brochure:** p. 25 bottom left. **Garmin International, Inc. brochure:** p. 25 bottom right. **Dean, Love, 1982,** *Reef Lights: Seaswept Lighthouses of the Florida Keys*, **Historic Key West Preservation Board, Key West:** p. 34. **Alastair Couper, ed., 1983,** *The Times Atlas of the Oceans*, **Van Nostrand, Reinhold, & Co.:** p. 37 right, redrawn by Sean Kelley. All other illustrations by Sean Kelley, except p. 7 and p. 37 left by Linda Harbin and Sean Kelley.

Contents

Preface

An Atlas of Maritime Florida was prepared as part of a multi-year project supported by the Coastal Management Program in Florida. The broad goal of the project was to prepare a management plan for the submerged cultural resources of Florida. While other components of the project involved developing tools that could be applied in local communities for locating, assessing, protecting, and interpreting shipwrecks, it became clear that no statewide plan could be devised until the historical and geographical context of shipwrecks was understood for the whole state. It was necessary to understand how the factors influencing the loss of vessels changed through history. Where were the traditional sailing and shipping routes? What were the sailing and navigation technologies that helped sailors avoid danger and arrive at their intended destinations? What were the principal hazards that resulted in shipwrecks and where were these most likely to occur? What aspects of commerce and industry determined the nature and routes of vessels in the different historical periods? What shipwrecks have been recorded or identified already and how are these distributed in space and time? All of these questions were relevant in preparing a plan for managing historic shipwreck sites throughout Florida.

This atlas is an exercise in learning answers to these questions, but it is also a way to bring this information to the public. Shipwrecks generate strong public interest which is readily developed and made more real by using shipwrecks as public historical resources. Shipwrecks can be brought to the public by means of shipwreck preserves, brochures, underwater guides, publications, volunteer projects, grant-supported survey projects, and university field schools. Each of these projects is a lesson in making these fascinating resources widely accessible. Providing opportunities to visit and explore shipwrecks promotes efforts to learn about and care for these exciting sites in our state's waters.

We are grateful to the Florida Coastal Management Program, originally managed by Florida Department of Environmental Regulation and later by Florida Department of Community Affairs. At the former office, our grant was administered by Jim Stoutamire; at the latter office we have had the support of Ralph Cantral and the able staff of the Program office. The National Oceanic and Atmospheric Administration has proved to be a most important source of funding for shipwreck resource management efforts in Florida. The program's support has meant the difference in Florida between progress and stagnation in an area that has traditionally been fraught with difficulty. Finally, a project of this nature involves little new or original work by the authors. Rather, it depends on collecting, organizing, and presenting the contributions of many people around the state. We have borrowed freely from standard references on Florida environment and history, as is evident from the bibliography at the back of the atlas. More importantly, we have benefited from the knowledge of sport divers, fishermen, and others who live, work, and play on the waters of Florida. Their participation and the results of their work make up the most important component of Florida's management scheme for historical shipwreck sites. We hope that this atlas will be interesting and useful to those who have already done so much to advance the practice of submerged cultural resource management, and that it will encourage even more of Florida's visitors and residents to become interested in these fascinating underwater time capsules.

Introduction

The story of Florida's maritime heritage is a long and continuous one. From the time of prehistoric coastal trade and the age of Spanish and French exploration, through the colonial, civil, and world wars and the modern period of international seaborne commerce, the Florida peninsula has been, and will continue to be, a strategic platform for maritime activities. Countless generations of people have sought Florida's shores in a myriad of water craft for a variety of aspirations. They continue to congregate at the water's edge, as culture after culture is drawn to the sea. Whether as a final destination, a transit point, or port of embarkation, Florida still retains its traditional maritime orientation in an age of space flight and satellite communications.

However, Florida's rich maritime history has not been well defined or described. The state's role as a cultural crossroads between the Atlantic, Caribbean, and Gulf of Mexico often is overlooked by residents and visitors alike. Yet, while the advent of railroads, highways, and air travel has changed the focus of other maritime communities, Florida remains perched on the frontier of the sea, which continues to shape its history.

This atlas is an attempt to bring together in one place basic information about Florida's maritime heritage in a format that encourages the reader to take a voyage through the past. The atlas presents the natural factors that affect shipping and navigation, such as

weather, currents, water depth, reefs and shoals, and the locations of inlets and rivers. These factors do not change very much over time, although their relative importance does change. The historical context of maritime activity is provided next. Each historical period is characterized by exploring trends in activities such as shipping, fishing, and recreation, and in maritime technology such as ship construction, propulsion, and navigation. Hazards to navigation are explored, as is the network of lighthouses along the coastline. Finally, ship losses and shipwrecks are presented to show patterns in time and space that formed as a result of the complicated interplay of natural and cultural factors.

Shipwrecks are among Florida's most exciting, but least understood historical sites. Surrounded by an aura of mystery and intrigue, shipwrecks fascinate us. The enigma of shipwrecks is often compounded by legends of treasure, easy to concoct but difficult to confirm. Florida's waters contain a vast variety of shipwreck sites, which represent frozen moments in time and pieces in the puzzle of the past. Yet, some people hold an unrealistic belief that every wreck is a Spanish galleon waiting to make its finder fabulously wealthy. It is hoped that this atlas will provide a greater understanding of these unique resources, and that it will encourage further studies of Florida's maritime history.

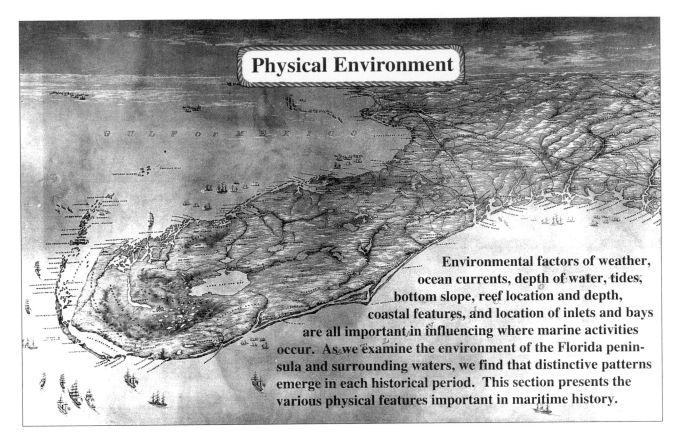

Physical Environment

Environmental factors of weather, ocean currents, depth of water, tides, bottom slope, reef location and depth, coastal features, and location of inlets and bays are all important in influencing where marine activities occur. As we examine the environment of the Florida peninsula and surrounding waters, we find that distinctive patterns emerge in each historical period. This section presents the various physical features important in maritime history.

Bathymetry and Shoreline

The Florida peninsula is an extension of the coastal plain of North America. It protrudes into the Caribbean, separating the Atlantic Ocean and the Gulf of Mexico. The shape and size of the peninsula are always changing, not only in minor ways along the local shores, but also in relation to the level of the sea. The size and configuration of the Florida peninsula at any time depends on the shape of the landform and the amount of water in the ocean basins. As shown in the map on page 3, the continental shelf landmass, of which modern Florida is the above-water part, has a steep slope on the Atlantic side and a shallow slope on the Gulf side. When the sea level was lower in Pleistocene times, Florida extended much farther into the Gulf than it does now. On the Atlantic side a change in sea level did not expose much more land. For ships under sail, the steep slopes of the Atlantic and the Keys were risky. Ships driven landward by storms or by poor navigation stood a greater chance of running aground on the sandy bottoms, or worse, on the fringing reefs.

The shorelines are not only navigational hazards to be avoided, they are also the destination of ships. Ships have little opportunity or need to approach land on an unbroken shore; an inlet, harbor, or sheltered bay is necessary to protect vessels and coastal settlements

from the forces of the open sea. The configuration of the coastline and its many openings play a major role in determining the location of settlements and ports. Inlets, those places where it is possible to cross from the open sea to a protected inland bay or river, are crucial locations for navigation. Inlets are protected by shallow bars and are often extremely hazardous. Before inlets were improved by dredging, by armoring against erosion, and by other aids to navigation, crossing the bar was often the responsibility of a local pilot who was familiar with the intricacies of depth, wind, and currents. Needless to say, many vessels in all historical periods have come to grief in and near inlets.

The energy regime of a shoreline is important in determining whether a ship that has run aground can be saved. High energy shorelines with strong currents or strong onshore winds, and those with steep slopes or fringing reefs and bars, may act to destroy a ship before it can be gotten free. On the other hand, a low energy shoreline with shallow slope and sandy or mud bottoms may be only a temporary inconvenience for a ship aground which may only need to wait for a proper tide. In general, the Atlantic and the Keys are more hostile to ships near the shoreline than is the Gulf of Mexico.

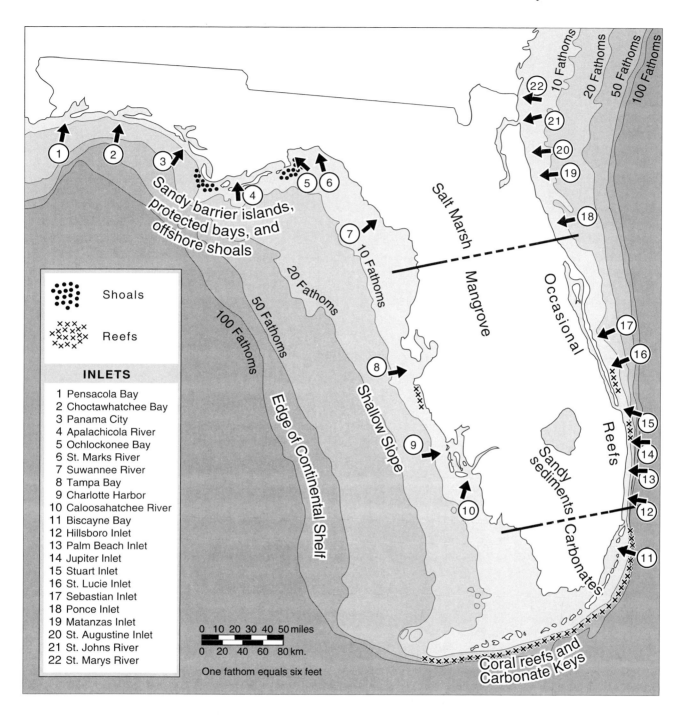

Shoals

Reefs

INLETS

1 Pensacola Bay
2 Choctawhatchee Bay
3 Panama City
4 Apalachicola River
5 Ochlockonee Bay
6 St. Marks River
7 Suwannee River
8 Tampa Bay
9 Charlotte Harbor
10 Caloosahatchee River
11 Biscayne Bay
12 Hillsboro Inlet
13 Palm Beach Inlet
14 Jupiter Inlet
15 Stuart Inlet
16 St. Lucie Inlet
17 Sebastian Inlet
18 Ponce Inlet
19 Matanzas Inlet
20 St. Augustine Inlet
21 St. Johns River
22 St. Marys River

0 10 20 30 40 50 miles
0 20 40 60 80 km.

One fathom equals six feet

Water depth and shoreline features were more important in the age of sail than during the late 19th and 20th centuries. As fuel propulsion gave vessels more power over the vagaries of wind and current, technologies of navigation, communication, and waterway maintenance also made the maritime voyage a safer prospect. The most hazardous aspects of depth and shore in the colonial periods were at the inlets associated with the state's earliest settlements, St. Augustine and Pensacola. Sailing vessels following the Gulf Stream along the lower east coast risked the violence of hurricanes during the fall season, as well as simple errors in navigation while threading the narrow Bahama Channel between the peninsula and the shallow Bahama banks. Similarly, those vessels sailing along the Florida Keys, both in Hawk Channel and outside the reef, ran the risk of wrecking on the treacherous coral reefs.

Winds and Currents

The weather is of vital importance to the mariner, since the wind and state of the sea directly affect navigation. In the age of sail, knowledge of favorable winds was of great importance, and accounting for ocean currents helped sailors to deduce their position at sea. Even fuel-powered vessels are profoundly affected by the movements of wind and sea. Information on prevailing winds and currents has gradually been gathered from ships' logs to produce piloting charts, which allow captains to select suitable routes, and to take advantage of anticipated conditions during passage. Advancements in meteorology continue to improve the efficiency and safety of maritime activity. Generally speaking, winds are named for the direction from which they come, currents for the direction in which they flow.

Land and sea breezes are often driven by an important physical property of water. The ocean's high *heat capacity* makes it change temperature much more slowly than dry land.

Daytime
As the sun rises, it begins to warm both land and sea. The sea reacts slowly, and as the day progresses, the land becomes much warmer. Air that comes in contact with this warm ground heats up and rises, while air over the ocean tends to remain cool and sink. This creates a circulation of air which, at ground level, is experienced as a sea breeze.

Nighttime
As the sun sets, both the ocean and the land have had all day to heat up, but without sunlight, the land rapidly loses its warmth. The ocean becomes a battery of warmth, slowly giving off heat throughout the night. The air rises over the ocean and sinks over the land, creating a land breeze.

Winds

Florida's winds are influenced by two systems: the North Atlantic Trade Winds and high and low pressure patterns that pass through the Westerly Wind Belt to the north. Wind circulation in the Gulf of Mexico is primarily clockwise around high-pressure areas. On the Atlantic coast, winds most frequently come out of the southeastern quadrant during the spring and summer, while in the fall and winter they blow from the southwestern quadrant. In the winter, the northern part of the state is strongly influenced by polar continental air masses moving southward towards the Gulf. These cold "northers" interact with the warm, moist sea air to form low-pressure centers accompanied by low clouds, rain, and fog. The southern part of the state continues to be influenced by trade wind patterns during the winter. Throughout the year, Florida's coastal winds are modified by the daily rhythm of land and sea breezes, as described at left.

Currents

Surface currents in the waters around Florida vary by season. During the winter, Gulf currents along the Panhandle run from west to east. As Gulf currents reach the Straits of Florida, they join with the main current of the Gulf of Mexico—the Loop Current—a clockwise circulation that is ultimately absorbed into the powerful Gulf Stream. The Gulf Stream, a remarkable ocean current that moves northward along the Atlantic coast, has been a major shipping artery from the Caribbean Basin into the North Atlantic. Its tremendous volume of water can be recognized by its deep indigo-blue color, which contrasts sharply with the dull green of the surrounding water. The Gulf Stream is frequently accompanied by squalls.

During the summer, currents of the Gulf coast of Florida generally run in opposite directions to their winter patterns. The currents along the Panhandle run from east to west, while the currents along the upper western coast run south to north. Below about 28 degrees of latitude, however, the currents are less consistent in their direction. This is due in part to the fact that the Loop Current recedes southward in the summer; its waters meet currents that are weakened where they join the Gulf Stream.

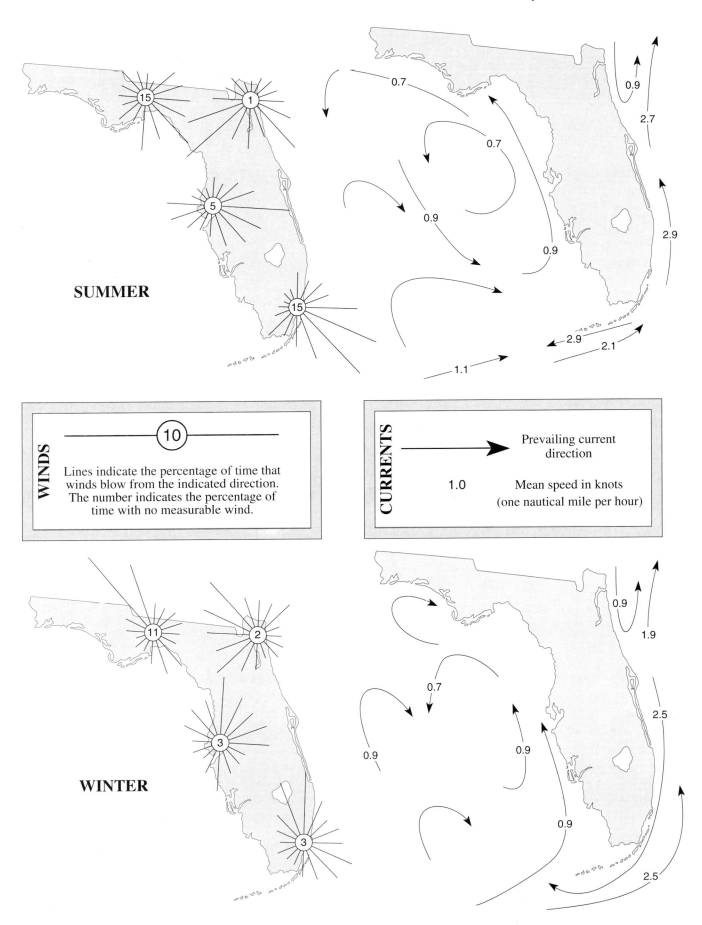

SUMMER

WINTER

WINDS

10

Lines indicate the percentage of time that winds blow from the indicated direction. The number indicates the percentage of time with no measurable wind.

CURRENTS

Prevailing current direction

1.0 Mean speed in knots (one nautical mile per hour)

Native Florida

The first people probably entered the Florida peninsula around 13,000 years ago, during the last glacial periods of the Pleistocene. Because so much sea water was locked up in the continental ice sheets, the sea was far below its current level and the Florida peninsula was twice its present size. As the global climate warmed, the sea level rose, reaching its modern level around 5,000 years ago. The archaeological remains of some of the first Floridians who lived along the coast are now submerged by the sea and in springs and rivers. People adapt to their environments, like all living things, and each Native American culture in Florida can be viewed as a way of making a living in a particular place at a particular time.

From the time of the first people, it is likely that the sea was important to native Floridians. We know that fish, shellfish, crustaceans, and other food sources were important along the coast and in the bays and rivers. When the sea level was lower, inland freshwater sources in springs and sinkholes, like Warm Mineral Springs and Little Salt Springs, were crucial to survival. Later, people relied on canoes for water transportation. The oldest canoe found in America, 5,000 years old, is from central Florida.

From this time until the European contact, the social and political organization of Florida natives increased in complexity. The Eastern Timucua tribes in northeast Florida relied heavily on the freshwater shellfish of the St. Johns River and of the coastal lagoons to supplement their agricultural production of corn, beans, and squash. The Western Timucua tribes were more agricultural. The Calusa of south Florida subsisted entirely on the rich estuarine resources of the mangrove coast of the Ten Thousand Islands area.

The map on page 7 shows a few of the most important coastal archaeological sites, such as Fort Walton, Crystal River, and Safety Harbor on the Gulf, and Turtle Mound on the Atlantic. These were all political and ceremonial centers of native Florida. Each regional center was supported by a complex of smaller settlements, much as our own rural and urban settlements are related today. The submerged sites on the map show the locations of the earliest native settlements. Their archaeological remains are now under water because of rising sea and water table levels.

Historical accounts and pictures show the maritime interests of Florida natives. There is tentative archaeological evidence for contact between the cultures

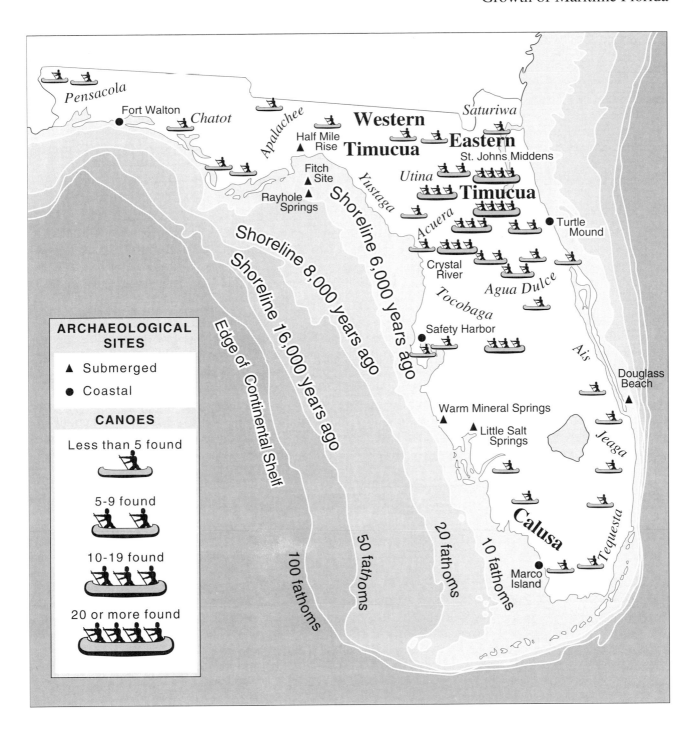

of Florida and the Caribbean islands prior to the arrival of the Europeans. After Europeans began to record the activities of the people inhabiting this "New World," there are frequent accounts of ocean canoe voyages between Florida and Cuba, and descriptions of these seaworthy vessels. It is likely that the most frequent and important use of watercraft by natives, however, was for coastal and inland travel. Florida natives had neither beasts of burden nor wheeled vehicles. With the advent of canoes came great improvements in the transportation of goods and people, and in the communication, trade, and interaction between native people of the entire southeastern United States.

The native tribes of Florida that met Europeans were extinct by the middle of the 18th century. They were victims of slavery, warfare, cultural disintegration, and, most importantly, European diseases against which they had no natural immunity.

European Exploration and Settlement

The European expansion to the Americas is called by some a discovery, by others an invasion. From either perspective, it was one of the most profound biological and cultural events in recorded history. For over three centuries, the economic wealth and the political power of European countries depended on their ability to exploit the vast natural and human resources of two continents which had not previously known the plow, the sail, the draft animal, gunpowder, or metal tools. Throughout this period, the sole means of communication and transportation of people and things between the two hemispheres was by sailing ship.

From the beginning of the 16th century and the first European contacts with Florida, through the early 1560s, the coasts of Florida were more important than the inland regions. A variety of unsuccessful attempts at colonization and settlement preceded the founding of St. Augustine in 1565. During this period, the key feature of Florida was the Gulf Stream off the Atlantic shore. Its strong currents propelled European vessels and fleets northward from the Caribbean ports through the treacherous Florida Channel to the latitude of South Carolina, where they left the coast and struck out across the Atlantic for the Azores and Spain.

Settlement of Florida by the Spanish through 1763 was a meager affair, restricted largely to the town of St. Augustine and two chains of Catholic missions running north and west from that center. The settlement was subsidized heavily by the Crown as a strategic outpost intended to protect the annual fleets carrying gold and silver back to Spain. St. Augustine was far from self-sufficient, yet it continued for two centuries to serve as a military center and port. Shipwrecked sailors along the Florida coast were often rescued by the St. Augustine garrison, and the city served as the religious, military, and political seat of Spanish Florida.

The beginning of the First Spanish Period was marked by a new ship type—the galleon, a small, fast, heavily armed sailing vessel that formed the foundation of the fleet system. Over time, galleons and their merchant consorts became larger and more heavily armed, but the principal technologies of ship construction, propulsion, and navigation remained essentially unchanged throughout this period. These ships were so successful that the Spanish transatlantic fleet system became the largest such enterprise until the Atlantic convoys of World War II. By 1600, the coasts were well known and charted, and accurate sailing instructions were widely available to Spanish mariners. Nonetheless, this maritime lifeline, however well-organized, remained at the mercy of hurricanes, especially in the narrow Florida Straits with its dangerous reefs and shoals. This was also the prime area of hurricane frequency; although the hurricane season was understood, as were the normal patterns of wind and weather, these killer storms could neither be predicted nor avoided.

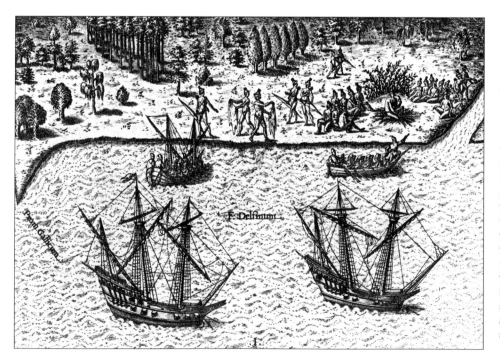

French Arrival in Florida
Engraving after Jacques le Moyne, an artist who accompanied a French expedition to Florida under René de Laudonnière in the year 1564. France sought to gain a foothold on this portion of the Atlantic coast to harass the convoys of her Spanish European rival, and sent a small Huguenot fleet under the command of Jean Ribaut, which landed in 1562 near the present site of St. Augustine. Although the French managed to establish a small fort, they were not able to hold the territory when a storm wrecked Ribaut's fleet, and the survivors were massacred by Spanish troops.

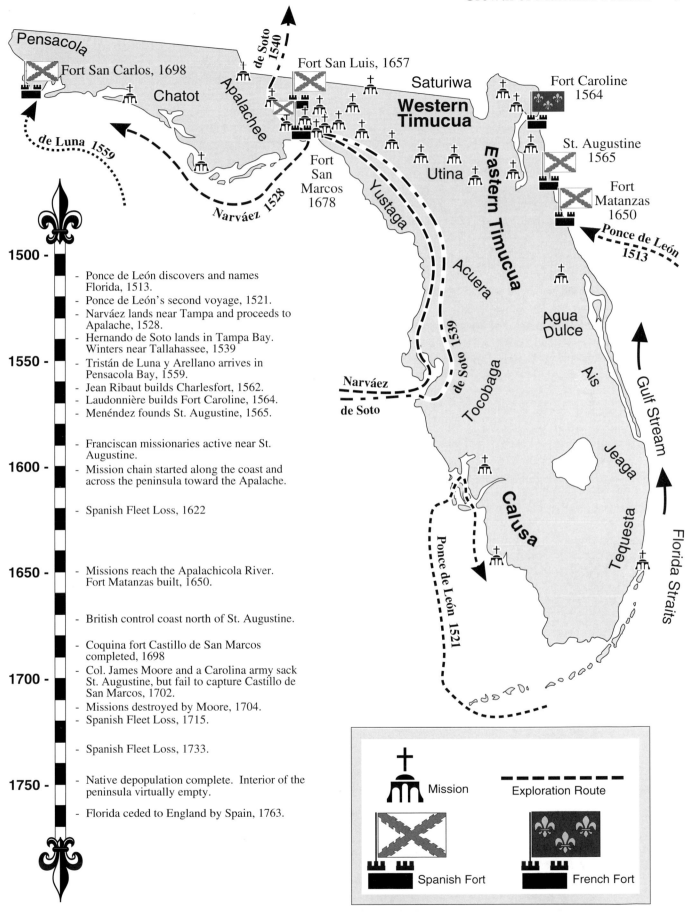

1500 -

- Ponce de León discovers and names Florida, 1513.
- Ponce de León's second voyage, 1521.
- Narváez lands near Tampa and proceeds to Apalache, 1528.
- Hernando de Soto lands in Tampa Bay. Winters near Tallahassee, 1539
- Tristán de Luna y Arellano arrives in Pensacola Bay, 1559.
- Jean Ribaut builds Charlesfort, 1562.
- Laudonnière builds Fort Caroline, 1564.
- Menéndez founds St. Augustine, 1565.

1550 -

- Franciscan missionaries active near St. Augustine.
- Mission chain started along the coast and across the peninsula toward the Apalache.

1600 -

- Spanish Fleet Loss, 1622

1650 -

- Missions reach the Apalachicola River. Fort Matanzas built, 1650.

- British control coast north of St. Augustine.

- Coquina fort Castillo de San Marcos completed, 1698
- Col. James Moore and a Carolina army sack St. Augustine, but fail to capture Castillo de San Marcos, 1702.

1700 -

- Missions destroyed by Moore, 1704.
- Spanish Fleet Loss, 1715.

- Spanish Fleet Loss, 1733.

1750 -

- Native depopulation complete. Interior of the peninsula virtually empty.

- Florida ceded to England by Spain, 1763.

Pensacola
Fort San Carlos, 1698
Chatot
Apalachee
Fort San Luis, 1657
Saturiwa
Western Timucua
Fort Caroline 1564
de Soto 1540
de Luna 1559
Narváez 1528
Fort San Marcos 1678
Yustaga
Utina
St. Augustine 1565
Fort Matanzas 1650
Ponce de León 1513
Eastern Timucua
Acuera
Agua Dulce
de Soto 1539
Narváez
de Soto
Tocobaga
Ais
Gulf Stream
Calusa
Jeaga
Tequesta
Florida Straits
Ponce de León 1521

✝ / ⛪ Mission
▬ ▬ ▬ Exploration Route
⚑ Spanish Fort
⚑ French Fort

Colonial Trade

In 1763, Spain relinquished her two-hundred-year control of Florida to Britain by the Treaty of Paris. The brief British Period (1763-1784) was marked by a new settlement strategy based on commercial plantations and intended to transform Florida into an economic asset, not a government subsidized liability. The New World gold and silver mines had been largely exhausted and the treasure fleet system had declined by the time of British occupation. In the two decades of that occupation, East and West Florida realized the colonial potential that had eluded Spain. St. Augustine's maritime strategic importance continued under the British, and Florida began to be viewed as a colony in the British sense, a unit of commercial production that could contribute to the wealth of the empire.

The East and West Florida colonies were incorporated into the British colonial mercantile shipping network. From Pensacola in West Florida and from St. Augustine on the east coast, such products as hides, indigo, sugar, timber, citrus, rice and naval stores were exported to other British colonies, and, for the first time, slaves were imported to Florida to provide labor for the plantations. This period also marked the opening of the interior by way of river and coastal navigation and by the construction of Florida's first road, the King's Road. The coast and the interior of Florida were accurately mapped in great detail as Britain sent some of its best surveyors to the new colony to chart the landscape and to lay out grants. The settled grants extended north and south from St. Augustine and surrounded Pensacola. They dramatically increased the European occupation of the interior and the accompanying water transportation along inland rivers and coastal bays.

Vessels of this period were mainly small frigates, brigs, schooners and sloops suitable for navigating the shallow inlets that provided the only access to the young ports. Pensacola and St. Augustine were garrisoned with troops, who were supported and transported by Royal Navy vessels, but the naval presence was relatively minor, compared to other British colonial ports such as Port Royal and Charleston. British Florida was threatened by Spain from its Mississippi stronghold on the west and by the American colonies on the north. Both ports became militarily important at the outbreak of the colonial revolution in 1776. By 1783, Britain had lost control of the Florida territory, ceding the land back to Spain. In the context of European geopolitics, Florida was little more than a pawn.

During the Second Spanish Period (1784-1821) and the following Territorial Period (1821-1845), Indian trade, plantation production, and naval stores continued to grow in importance. Products became relatively more important in quantity and economic value, with regular maritime trade established between Florida, the rest of the Eastern seaboard, and with French settlements on the Gulf coast. The interior of the peninsula remained largely unsettled, but such ports as Fernandina, Jacksonville, Tampa, St. Marks, St. Joe and Apalachicola began to transport timber and cotton on a large scale to northern states and to Europe.

With the advent of steam propulsion at the end of the 1820s, a slow but steady growth of improved navigation and shipping expanded throughout Florida. The territory was linked economically to the major southeast ports of Savannah and Charleston, and coastal transportation, spurred by the Second Seminole War, integrated the east and west coast Florida ports. Aids to navigation were constructed in the most hazardous areas along reefs and shoals, and very detailed coastal charts were produced by the federal government.

Camp Volusia of Fort Barnwell on the St. Johns
One of the early military encampments of the interior, accessible only by boat on the St. Johns River.

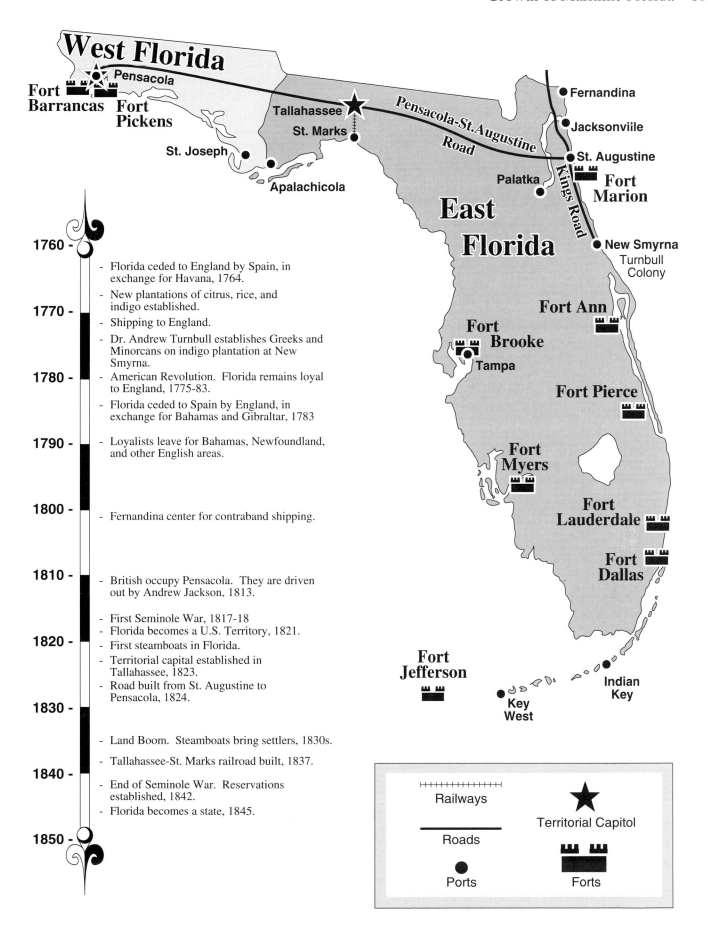

West Florida
Pensacola
Fort Barrancas   Fort Pickens
Tallahassee
St. Marks
Pensacola-St. Augustine Road
Fernandina
Jacksonviile
St. Augustine
Palatka
Kings Road
Fort Marion
St. Joseph
Apalachicola
East Florida
New Smyrna
Turnbull Colony
Fort Ann
Fort Brooke
Tampa
Fort Pierce
Fort Myers
Fort Lauderdale
Fort Dallas
Fort Jefferson
Indian Key
Key West

1760 –

- Florida ceded to England by Spain, in exchange for Havana, 1764.
- New plantations of citrus, rice, and indigo established.
- Shipping to England.

1770 –

- Dr. Andrew Turnbull establishes Greeks and Minorcans on indigo plantation at New Smyrna.

1780 –

- American Revolution. Florida remains loyal to England, 1775-83.
- Florida ceded to Spain by England, in exchange for Bahamas and Gibraltar, 1783

1790 –

- Loyalists leave for Bahamas, Newfoundland, and other English areas.

1800 –

- Fernandina center for contraband shipping.

1810 –

- British occupy Pensacola. They are driven out by Andrew Jackson, 1813.

1820 –

- First Seminole War, 1817-18
- Florida becomes a U.S. Territory, 1821.
- First steamboats in Florida.
- Territorial capital established in Tallahassee, 1823.
- Road built from St. Augustine to Pensacola, 1824.

1830 –

- Land Boom. Steamboats bring settlers, 1830s.
- Tallahassee-St. Marks railroad built, 1837.

1840 –

- End of Seminole War. Reservations established, 1842.
- Florida becomes a state, 1845.

1850 –

+++++++++++++++
Railways

⭐
Territorial Capitol

Roads

● Ports

Forts

Expansion of Maritime Commerce

Florida's new status as a state beginning in 1845 strengthened economic and political stability and allowed a rapid development of commerce, primarily in the northern part of the state. The principal ports of Jacksonville, Fernandina, St. Marks, Apalachicola and Pensacola shipped vast cargoes of timber, naval stores, cotton, and citrus. The Atlantic and Gulf coasts were linked by rail from Fernandina to Cedar Key, providing improved transportation of inland products to ports.

By the beginning of the Civil War, Florida had become an important maritime state; her exports reached principal Atlantic, Caribbean, and European markets. Although blockaded by the Union Navy, Florida ports became important to the Confederate war effort by serving blockade runners, who exchanged Florida products for supplies required by the Confederacy to carry on the war. In the "three-cornered trade," northern manufactured goods were ultimately exchanged for southern agricultural and timber products by way of Bahamian merchants. The established ports were joined by Jupiter on the Atlantic coast and Cedar Key on the Gulf coast as the principal ports of the blockade-running trade. Blockade runners as well as Union and Confederate vessels were casualties of the conflict, but the most significant naval engagements of the Civil War occurred along the middle Atlantic states.

During Reconstruction, the interior and southern part of the Florida peninsula opened for development with the establishment of inland steam navigation on the St. Johns River and the growth of such ports as Ft. Myers and Tampa. The golden age of steamboats on the St. Johns River saw regular passenger and cargo service as far south as the center of the state through the middle 1880s. Jacksonville became the principal deep-water Florida port, with oceangoing steam connections to international ports, as well as rail connections throughout the rich Florida interior. Tampa similarly served the Caribbean trade with important rail connections. The discovery of phosphate southeast of Tampa led to significant artificial improvements to the bay, channel, and wharves. Hundreds of thousands of tons of phosphate were shipped from Tampa annually in the late 1880s.

Coastal communities had long relied on fish and shellfish for local use and some export, but large quantities of perishable seafood could not be shipped by rail until the invention of ice machinery. This development increased the interior market dramatically, and substantial commercial fisheries developed in Florida. The premier rail lines of Plant on the west coast and Flagler on the east coast were responsible for the development of modern Florida seaports at Tampa and Miami.

The once treacherous shallow bars and changing channels of the Florida inlets were yielding to dredging, armoring, and continued maintenance. The federal government, along with port authorities, encouraged by local businesses, provided the facilities and organization necessary for reliable shipping service. The U.S. Army Corps of Engineers and the U.S. Coast Survey provided improvements in channels and harbors as well as highly accurate charts and maps of navigable waters. As the hazards to navigation were reduced, the willingness of shipping companies to use Florida ports increased. Communication and weather prediction remained unsophisticated. Hurricanes could not be predicted and aid for ships in distress was limited to that provided by passing vessels or land observers.

During the Spanish-American War at the close of the century, the U.S. Navy and Army had taken advantage of Florida's strategic location in the Caribbean. Tens of thousands of troops and their supplies embarked from Tampa in the largest invasion force yet to leave American soil. Virtually overnight, Key West became a major naval base serving coal-powered U.S. warships in the invasion of Cuba.

Chattahoochee on the St. Johns River near Georgetown, early 1890s.

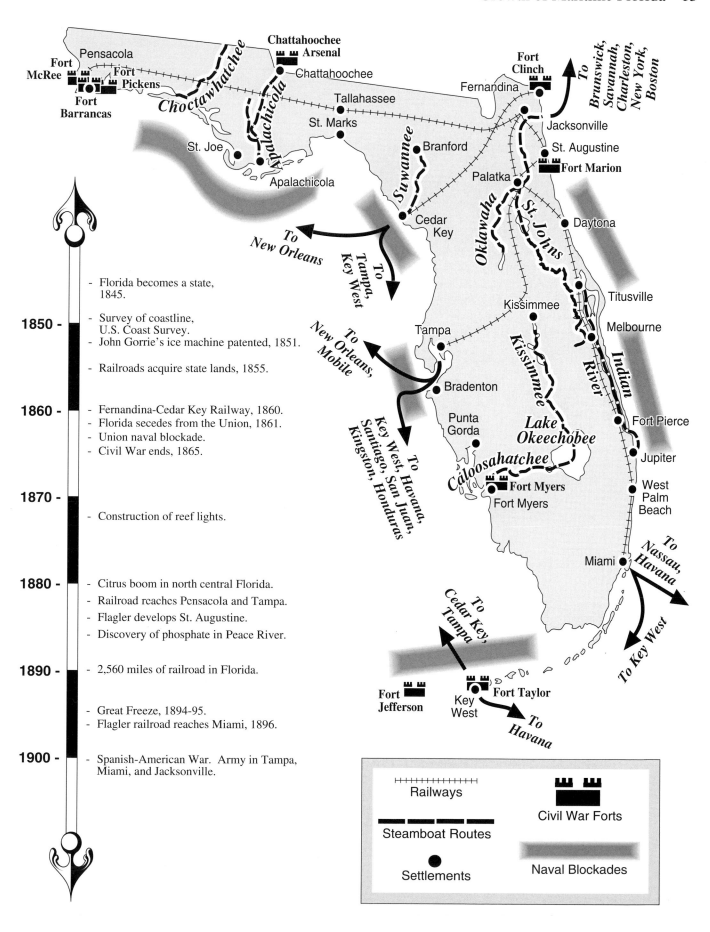

Fort McRee
Pensacola
Fort Pickens
Fort Barrancas
Choctawhatchee
Chattahoochee Arsenal
Chattahoochee
Tallahassee
St. Marks
Apalachicola
St. Joe
Apalachicola
Suwannee
Branford
Cedar Key
Fort Clinch
Fernandina
Jacksonville
St. Augustine
Fort Marion
Palatka
Oklawaha
St. Johns
Daytona
Titusville
Melbourne
Indian River
Kissimmee
Kissimmee
Lake Okeechóbee
Caloosahatchee
Fort Myers
Fort Myers
Punta Gorda
Bradenton
Tampa
Fort Pierce
Jupiter
West Palm Beach
Miami
Fort Jefferson
Key West
Fort Taylor

To Brunswick, Savannah, Charleston, New York, Boston
To New Orleans
To Tampa, Key West
To New Orleans, Mobile
To Key West, Havana, Santiago, San Juan, Kingston, Honduras
To Nassau, Havana
To Key West
To Cedar Key, Tampa
To Havana

- Florida becomes a state, 1845.
1850 -
- Survey of coastline, U.S. Coast Survey.
- John Gorrie's ice machine patented, 1851.
- Railroads acquire state lands, 1855.

1860 -
- Fernandina-Cedar Key Railway, 1860.
- Florida secedes from the Union, 1861.
- Union naval blockade.
- Civil War ends, 1865.

1870 -
- Construction of reef lights.

1880 -
- Citrus boom in north central Florida.
- Railroad reaches Pensacola and Tampa.
- Flagler develops St. Augustine.
- Discovery of phosphate in Peace River.

1890 -
- 2,560 miles of railroad in Florida.
- Great Freeze, 1894-95.
- Flagler railroad reaches Miami, 1896.

1900 -
- Spanish-American War. Army in Tampa, Miami, and Jacksonville.

+++++++++++ Railways
━━ ━━ ━━ Steamboat Routes
● Settlements
Civil War Forts
Naval Blockades

Modern Maritime Industry

By the beginning of the 20th century, Florida had become thoroughly incorporated into the global maritime system. Her ports could accommodate international trade, and her exports were valued in foreign as well as national markets. The first half of the century brought about sweeping changes in the technology of navigation. Wireless telegraph, in wide use by World War I, provided the first ship-to-shore and ship-to-ship communication beyond the range of sight. For the first time, ships could be notified of hazards at sea, such as storms, and could request aid when in distress. Radio beacons could provide a rough locational fix near the coast, and could improve navigation at night and in bad weather. Shortwave radio allowed communication far at sea by code as well as voice. Regular and accurate radio broadcasts of weather conditions allowed ships at sea to prepare for or avoid dangerous storms. By the end of World War II, well-equipped ocean-going vessels could accurately determine their positions, follow designated courses, successfully avoid obstacles and each other, and have full knowledge of sea and weather conditions all along their routes.

Steam boilers switched from coal to oil, a cleaner-burning and more efficient fuel. Steel replaced iron in the ships' structure and steel hulls became standard for most vessel types. Ships were built more quickly and cheaply with steel and the size of ships increased dramatically. During the war effort, modern assembly-line production techniques turned out new warships on a daily basis. While Florida ports played a relatively minor role in World War II, and while military naval engagements occurred far from the American coasts, northeast Florida was the location of a successful submarine campaign against Allied merchant shipping.

In the second half of the 20th century, Florida's population grew dramatically as did her place in international trade and commerce. Regular and efficient air service had taken over much of the passenger trade from ships, but transportation of commercial cargo continued to support an expanding maritime network. The port of Miami replaced Havana as the hub of Caribbean commerce, and Miami eventually came to resemble a Latin city more than an Anglo one. Hundreds of vessels brought political and economic refugees from Cuba, Haiti and other Caribbean countries. Tragically, many were lost on the way.

As airlines replaced passenger ships for travel across the oceans, the large vessels began to be refitted as cruise ships. In the 1960s and 1970s the cruise industry exploded in Florida; today people come from around the world to embark on cruise ships from Florida ports. Trips range from overnight cruises to the Bahamas to voyages around the world.

The largest number of boats in Florida are pleasure boats. In certain coastal residential developments with waterfront access, virtually every home has a boat. Marinas and waterways are overcrowded with high-powered pleasure boats. Sport fishermen, jet skiers, power boaters, sail boaters, and water-skiers all compete for a piece of the open water each weekend. The primary role of water transportation in our state's history has been supplanted by air and land transportation; at the same time, our waterways have become playgrounds for every kind of vessel available, from windsurfing boards to yachts.

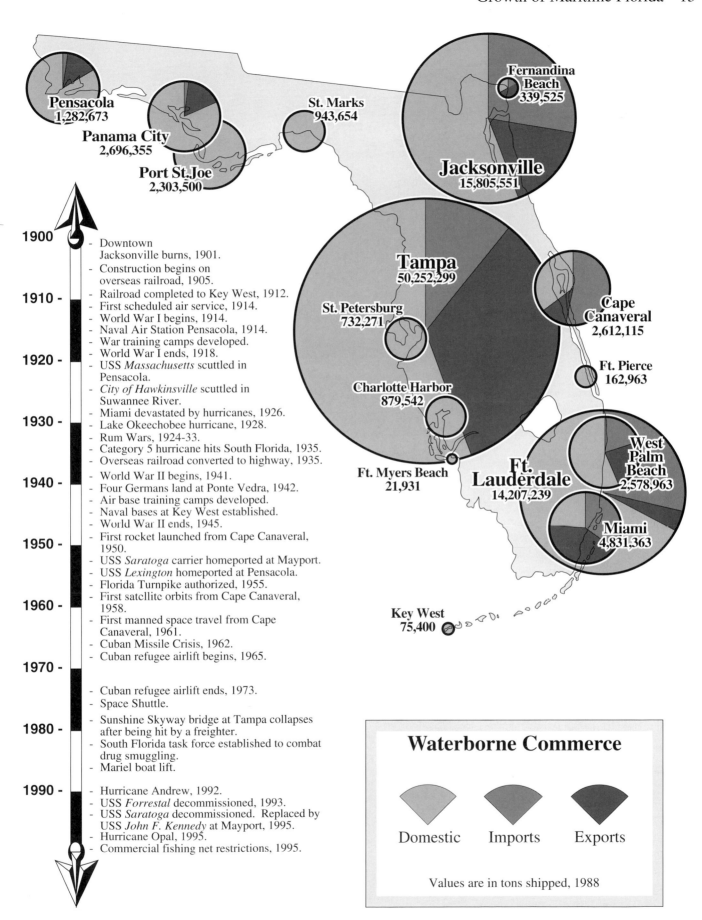

Pensacola
1,282,673

Panama City
2,696,355

Port St.Joe
2,303,500

St. Marks
943,654

Fernandina
Beach
339,525

Jacksonville
15,805,551

Tampa
50,252,299

St. Petersburg
732,271

Cape
Canaveral
2,612,115

Ft. Pierce
162,963

Charlotte Harbor
879,542

Ft. Myers Beach
21,931

Ft.
Lauderdale
14,207,239

West
Palm
Beach
2,578,963

Miami
4,831,363

Key West
75,400

1900
- Downtown Jacksonville burns, 1901.
- Construction begins on overseas railroad, 1905.
1910 -
- Railroad completed to Key West, 1912.
- First scheduled air service, 1914.
- World War I begins, 1914.
- Naval Air Station Pensacola, 1914.
- War training camps developed.
1920 -
- World War I ends, 1918.
- USS *Massachusetts* scuttled in Pensacola.
- *City of Hawkinsville* scuttled in Suwannee River.
- Miami devastated by hurricanes, 1926.
1930 -
- Lake Okeechobee hurricane, 1928.
- Rum Wars, 1924-33.
- Category 5 hurricane hits South Florida, 1935.
- Overseas railroad converted to highway, 1935.
1940 -
- World War II begins, 1941.
- Four Germans land at Ponte Vedra, 1942.
- Air base training camps developed.
- Naval bases at Key West established.
- World War II ends, 1945.
1950 -
- First rocket launched from Cape Canaveral, 1950.
- USS *Saratoga* carrier homeported at Mayport.
- USS *Lexington* homeported at Pensacola.
- Florida Turnpike authorized, 1955.
1960 -
- First satellite orbits from Cape Canaveral, 1958.
- First manned space travel from Cape Canaveral, 1961.
- Cuban Missile Crisis, 1962.
- Cuban refugee airlift begins, 1965.
1970 -
- Cuban refugee airlift ends, 1973.
- Space Shuttle.
1980 -
- Sunshine Skyway bridge at Tampa collapses after being hit by a freighter.
- South Florida task force established to combat drug smuggling.
- Mariel boat lift.
1990 -
- Hurricane Andrew, 1992.
- USS *Forrestal* decommissioned, 1993.
- USS *Saratoga* decommissioned. Replaced by USS *John F. Kennedy* at Mayport, 1995.
- Hurricane Opal, 1995.
- Commercial fishing net restrictions, 1995.

Waterborne Commerce

Domestic   Imports   Exports

Values are in tons shipped, 1988

Wrecking

For hundreds of years, unlucky vessels routinely ran aground on Florida's reefs. The salvage of ships' cargos, called "wrecking," became profitable for small groups of determined sailors. The first wreckers were the Calusa Indians, who preyed on commerce stranded off the Florida Keys until 1763, when they were removed to Cuba at the end of the first Spanish occupation of Florida. The new British colony of Florida attracted wreckers from the Bahamas, who became established at locations along the Keys with good harbors and fresh water, close to dangerous sections of the reef. By the time the United States acquired Florida in 1821, American merchants recognized the value of Key West as a strategic port. All vessels sailing to and from the Gulf of Mexico had to pass along the dangerous Florida Keys; inevitably, many ran aground or were wrecked on the reefs. Key West became an official port of entry and salvage collection depot, and large wrecking vessels arrived to make the port their home. A Superior Court established in 1828 gave Key West jurisdiction over all salvage collected between Port Charlotte and Indian River. By 1847, a District Court was created, and wrecking became a well-regulated enterprise with licensed vessels and strict legal controls.

Wrecking was a risky business. Owners of wrecking vessels wagered their investment on the chance to salvage profitable wrecks; crews gambled their lives for a share in the potential proceeds. The first salvor to board the stricken ship was required to deliver a copy of his license and the court's rules to its captain, who had the right to refuse assistance, or to employ any vessel he chose to help him. Otherwise, the captain of the first wrecker on the scene became the wreck master, and took charge of the salvage. When recovered, property was taken into Key West, where its value was appraised and where the district judge awarded a percentage to the salvor to be paid in kind or from the proceeds of sale. No reward was made for the saving of lives.

One-half of the total award went to the wrecking vessel and its owner; the other half was divided among the crew into as many shares as there were men on board.

Typical vessels in the wrecking business were fast, shallow-draft sloops and schooners, ranging from 10 to 100 tons in burden. Their numbers on the Florida reef increased from 20 in 1835, to 27 in 1851, then to 57 licensed vessels in 1858. But as the first formal coastal survey of the reefs and keys began in 1849, and a system of lighthouses was constructed along the reef, the number of shipwrecks began to decline. The business of wrecking, however, continued into the next century; between 1900 and 1910, more than $220,000 salvage was awarded by court decree, and more than $100,000 was paid for claims out of court. Finally, in December 1921, a hundred years after Florida became a United States territory, the wrecking register of the Key West District Court was closed.

Smuggling

With over 8,000 miles of shoreline, Florida has always been at the crossroads of maritime smuggling. Florida's many islands, rivers, and bays are ideal landing places for contraband cargos. Waterborne games of hide-and-seek have been played throughout the state's maritime history; in this century, the smuggling of alcohol and drugs by sea placed Florida in the forefront of this clandestine trade.

The National Prohibition Act of 1919, which outlawed the manufacture and sale of alcohol in the United States, drew smugglers to Florida's shores in old schooners, rusty tramp steamers, former gunboats, and onetime luxury yachts flying many flags. Bringing rum and similar spirits from Cuba, Jamaica, and other islands to just outside the three-mile territorial limit, the contraband merchants rode at anchor, holds open wide, ready to do business with anyone who would come out to buy their wares.

This armada of strange vessels was called Rum Row. Delivery to shore was carried out by a "sunset fleet" of small craft, which operated at night. Convoys of trucks hauled the landed contraband towards metropolitan areas, where local bootleggers took over distribution. Profits were enormous. The U.S. Coast Guard played a cat-and-mouse game with the rum smugglers. At first, naval relics of the Spanish-American War were used to chase the "sunset fleet," but, beginning in 1924, recommissioned destroyers joined fast picket boats, especially designed for stealth and speed. As syndicates moved into the contraband trade, the game accelerated into a naval war. An Offshore Patrol Force, with new steel-hulled, long-range boats, eventually chased the "rummies" from the seas, as syndicates set up their own illicit distilleries ashore to compete with southern moonshine for the customer's dollar. Repeal of Prohibition in 1933 eventually ended the rum wars at sea.

Just as Florida's geographic position near rum-producing countries made the peninsula a convenient smuggling conduit, its proximity to source countries for narcotics caused the state to become a haven for drug smugglers in the 1970s and 1980s. Cocaine from Colombia and marijuana from Jamaica were the principal drugs smuggled into Florida by a variety of maritime routes, and by an increasing number of small airplanes. Florida became the scene of intense competition between smugglers while gang warfare and drug-related assassinations proliferated. In 1982 a South Florida Task Force combined agencies such as Customs, the FBI, and the Drug Enforcement Agency to work with the Coast Guard to patrol the air and sea lanes around Florida. High-speed cutters and jet airplanes were added to the force, as were low-profile offshore racing boats and military helicopters armed with 30-million candle-power spotlights.

The U.S. government spent hundreds of millions of dollars in support of the South Florida Task Force, which confiscated hundreds of thousands of pounds of smuggled drugs and millions of dollars' worth of boats, airplanes, cars, trucks, and other property. Hundreds of people, including those who were involved in laundering drug money, were captured and sent to prison; yet, hundreds of others escaped detection and apprehension, and the smuggling of narcotics continues to be a significant maritime industry in Florida today, despite the efforts of law enforcement.

Liquor captured by a Florida Sheriff during Prohibition.

Lumber

The cutting of trees for lumber has been one of Florida's most important maritime-related enterprises. The peninsula's vast quantity of timber was first used by native Floridians, who felled trees by burning, and shaped their canoes by charring the logs with fire and scraping them with flint. Early European explorers quickly recognized the importance of Florida lumber in the building of ships; Narváez constructed his boats on the Apalachee coast in 1528, and Menéndez built a ship at St. Augustine that sailed back to Spain.

Live oak trees were highly valued for shipbuilding, since their naturally curved hardwood limbs made ideal framing and knees, while straight trunks were used for keels and sternposts. Camps of live oak cutters were established during the colonial period on Florida's bays, inlets, and rivers. The lumber trade became important during the Territorial Period, as early saw mills were established in the St. Johns River and Pensacola Bay regions. The Pensacola Navy Yard, established in 1826, included a naval live oak plantation for growing and harvesting timbers for shipbuilding and repair. The federal government's interest in Florida's timber resources was demonstrated by the establishment of the Apalachicola, Ocala, and Osceola National Forests.

The growing use of iron in shipbuilding made live oak less important, and pine and cypress became the primary species in Florida's lumber trade; however, for a short time, the harvesting of red cedar became an important industry, particularly at Cedar Key. Aside from its use as timber, pine was used in the production of naval stores, which are turpentine, rosin, and byproducts of pitch and tar, all distilled from pine resin.

Many of the towns in Florida, especially in the northern counties, were built around lumber mills; by the mid-1800s water power had been replaced by steam power, and circular saws were accompanied by planing machinery to produce high-grade board lumber. The first and most important revenue of most of Florida's railroads came from hauling logs, lumber, and crossties to build more railroads. The yellow and pitch pine industry, centered in West Florida, reached a peak at the turn of the century; the port of Pensacola had become the largest exporter in the United States. By steamer and schooner, the ports of Fernandina and Jacksonville shipped large quantities of timber and crossties that were used to construct the Panama Canal and railroad, the Cuba railroad, and to maintain the major railroads of New England.

Lumber ready for shipment out of Pensacola.

Marine Recreation

By the 1870s the pleasant climate and medicinal qualities of Florida's mineral springs, such as White Springs and Silver Springs, had begun to attract visitors seeking to comfort the sicknesses associated with weaknesses in their lungs, bones, and muscles. Steamboat tours along the many rivers and lakes in north and central Florida were frequented by hunting and fishing enthusiasts, notably along the St. Johns River. With the addition of railroad linkages to the northern United States in the 1880s, luxury hotels began to crop up, attracting many wealthy vacationers. A new type of tourism based on more indulgent activities like yachting allowed growth in the southern coasts of the state.

The Florida peninsula has 1,200 miles of coastline, 7,700 lakes over 10 acres in size, nearly 300 springs, and approximately 4,500 islands of at least 10 acres which draw residents and tourists alike to the high-quality waters of the state. This provides a large array of opportunities for water-oriented activities and recreational fishing. Freshwater lakes offer many species such as bream, catfish, and most notably the largemouth bass. In the coastal waters, tarpon, cobia, and king mackeral are favorites.

Steamboat *Marion* around 1874. Steamboats provided commercial and passenger transportation between interior ports before roads and railroads were well developed. They were also an important part of the early tourist trade, bringing northern visitors into the interior rivers and providing a wilderness experience for urban tourists.

Windsurfing. The recreational use of water craft has been taken to its simplest individual form in the sailboard and the jet-ski. These vessels carry neither crew nor cargo, only a captain. They represent the most democratic form of maritime recreation—personal access to every body of water.

Where the Gulf Stream runs near the southeast shoreline of Florida, sailfish and marlin seekers charter fishing boat trips.

Fishing is not the only marine recreation pursued in Florida's waters. The coral reefs along the seaward side of the Florida Keys are the only ones in the continental U.S. and are home to over 200 species of fish and 50 species of coral, making it a paradise for scuba divers and snorkelers. John Pennekamp Coral Reef State Park is almost completely underwater, and with over one million visitors annually, is the most popular recreational location in the state. Scuba diving is also popular in the freshwater springs within the state because of underwater cavern formations.

Boating activities are extremely popular. Canoeists enjoy the many peaceful rivers and streams crisscrossing the state while sailing and water-skiing are pursued in the lakes and coastal areas. Cruise ships touring the Caribbean accommodate nearly seven million passengers each year from six seaports (Canaveral, Ft. Lauderdale, Miami, Palm Beach, Key West, St. Petersburg, and Tampa), and a variety of pleasure craft cruise the scenic intracoastal waterway that runs along much of the state's coast.

The great diversity of unique environments along the inland lakes, rivers, and springs, and on Florida's coastal waters offers endless opportunities for exploration and enjoyment.

Commercial Fishing

The abundance of Florida's marine life at the time when Europeans first arrived is well documented. Archaeological study of native Indian sites indicates a heavy reliance on marine resources for food, most notably in the southern half of the state, where the remains of sea turtle, clam, oyster, manatee, conch, and several fish species have been found. Along the coasts, shells and shark's teeth were used to make tools, weapons, and decorative objects.

Spanish settlers had little interest in commercial exploitation of marine resources, and during the British occupation in the late 18th century, there was no development of fishing as a profitable industry. Fishermen from Cuba and the Bahamas, who came to Florida twice a year for fish and green turtles, were the primary agents of fishing activity until the middle of the 19th century. Working amicably along with the local Indians, they built huts along Charlotte Harbor and the Florida Keys to produce dried fish for a large market based in Havana.

By the 1830s, the Bahamians had been replaced in the Keys by fishermen from the northern states and St. Augustine who began delivering live reef fish to Havana by keeping them in live wells built into the boat's hull. This limited the quantity and range of shipments and created a great amount of waste, since fish killed or damaged during rough seas were discarded.

Key West thrived as a fishing community even after the Cuban Revolution in 1868 restricted trade. This decline was offset by an increase in the area's sponge fishing, and a range from Key West to St. John's Pass became regionally significant to the fishing industry. Oysters were also a major regional product harvested south from Apalachicola Bay to the Anclote Keys.

Beginning in 1869, a thriving red snapper market in Pensacola took advantage of railroad connections to New Orleans. Later, with the availability of ice, access to the north and west was greatly increased, and Florida's fishermen were able to tap into the high demand for fresh fish and oysters that had developed in those regions. Smacks (large schooners of 50-60 tons) were primarily used at sea, while chings, smaller (5-20 ton) vessels, sailed along the coast to Tampa.

Mullet was taken in large quantities from the Tampa Bay and Charlotte Harbor areas, and by 1896, after railroad lines were built to Miami, the east coast along the Indian River had developed into an important mullet fishery source. Florida was ranked tenth in the nation for commercial fisheries in 1896, and sponging was the most valuable fishing industry in the state, with a third of total sales, followed by mullet, red snapper, oysters, and sea trout.

Shrimping began around the turn of the century on the east coast with rapid growth occurring after the introduction of the otter trawl in 1912. This type of net allowed dragging in deep water and at the heaviest concentrations of shrimp. Production declines in the late 1940s prompted a search that led to the 1950 discovery of pink shrimp in the Dry Tortugas. This region brought in fifteen million pounds the first season, displacing Apalachicola as Florida's primary Gulf-coast shrimping center, and shrimp, rather than mullet, became the major commercial seafood catch for the whole state.

Currently Florida's most valuable commercial species is still shrimp, accounting for 40% of all sales, followed by spiny lobster, crab (blue and stone), and red snapper. The west coast has gained dominance over time, especially Tampa Bay and Apalachicola Bay. Oysters, scallops, and finfish (from which fishmeal is produced) are other important catches, and most of the state's commercial fishing is highly dependent upon the delicate ecosystems surrounding the coastline. Blue crab, grouper, and red snapper are widely distributed along the coasts, but several other estuarine-dependent species of commercial importance are still found mainly in regionalized pockets. In 1995 Florida voters approved a constitutional amendment to limit the size of fishing nets allowed in state waters.

Historic Trade

With thousands of miles of coastline, and no point more than sixty miles from sea water, Florida has always depended on maritime trade. Coastal and riverine networks were used by native canoes for aboriginal trade before the arrival of Europeans. Fortified Spanish settlements at St. Augustine, St. Marks, and Pensacola were connected by native trails on land, but their principal strategic locations on the Gulf and Atlantic linked them by sea to Havana. During the Spanish mission period, the Apalachee region supplied maize, grains, and livestock through the port of St. Marks to Havana and St. Augustine, which suffered from a chronic shortage of foodstuffs. The garrison at Pensacola, established to counter French designs in the region, was linked by sea with Mexico.

The British occupation of Florida prompted the establishment of colonial plantations which produced rice, indigo, sugar, and citrus along the St. Johns River. St. Augustine became the economic center of the colony and was a port of entry for English goods that were transshipped from Charleston, which had a deeper harbor. West Florida was considered to have great potential as a fishery, for naval stores, and as a source of lumber and provisions for the Caribbean sugar islands. The slave trade also became important, and business with local Indians concentrated on the fur trade. A large amount of illegal trade with Spanish Louisiana and Mexico was carried on from Pensacola. By the time of the American Revolution, a packet system of shipping mail, passengers and cargo had been introduced to the colony. During the Second Spanish Period (1783-1821), West Florida assumed prominence as vast amounts of timber and turpentine were exported to Europe. The British firm, Panton, Leslie and Company, monopolized the Indian trade by exchanging European-made guns, powder, and flint for furs. In East Florida, Fernandina became a prosperous port, while St. Augustine dwindled in economic importance.

In 1821, Florida was ceded to the United States by Spain; Americans took over vacant citrus groves along the St. Johns River, drained swamps, and expanded plantations. For a brief period St. Augustine regained its prominence in coastal trade with northern markets; but soon the new port of Jacksonville began to assume control over much of this shipping. In the Gulf, St. Marks, St. Joseph, and Apalachicola became important cotton exporters, and Tampa's birth as a seaport came about due to its strategic location as a supply depot in the Seminole wars. In Pensacola, the federal government built 1,000 feet of wharfage for ships to dock in the deep-water port. By the 1850s, new railroads connected North Florida's principal ports with the interior; citrus, cotton, and forest products, bound to northern or overseas destinations, filled the docks.

During the Civil War, Florida's ports became important to the Confederacy. Although blockaded by the federal navy, St. Marks, Cedar Key, and Tampa along the Gulf, and Fernandina, St. Augustine, and Jupiter Inlet on the Atlantic were active transit points for ships which slipped through the blockade by night. The blockade runners took cotton, tobacco, and turpentine in exchange for medical supplies, manufactured goods, and munitions needed by the South. Reconstruction after the war prompted the gradual development of central and south Florida, with the St. Johns River port of Jacksonville as the gateway. Railroads, such as those built by Henry Plant from Jacksonville to Tampa, and by Flagler along the east coast, began to accelerate settlement, trade and tourism. By the turn of the century, Florida had become a maritime crossroads between the United States, Central and South America, and Europe.

The docks at Pensacola.

Modern Trade

Florida's economy has undergone dramatic changes in the last two decades. While agriculture, tourism, and construction continue to play important roles in the state economy, the industrial sector has experienced enormous growth. A reflection of this industrialization is the growth of the state's international trade, which has had a significant impact on Florida's economy. Florida's destiny has always been international. But more than ever before, the economic well-being of Florida is linked to the world economy. Through expanding international trade, tourism, financial markets, and investment opportunities, Florida is at the crossroads of the global marketplace. The modern expansion of Florida's international trade resulted from a number of factors, such as a reduction in trade barriers, advancements in communications technology, and the changing economic relationship between industrial and developing nations.

Florida's position at the crossroads of the Western Hemisphere, the Atlantic, and the Gulf also explains its recent growth and foretells its future role in the increasing movements of international goods, services, and ideas. In addition, Florida's cultural diversity gives it competitive advantages over other states, especially in Latin America and the Caribbean, which are areas of market competition between the United States and other countries. As could be expected, Florida's major export markets have been traditionally located in these regions,

accounting for about three-fourths of the state's export sales in the past. Venezuela remains one of Florida's most important customers, as does Brazil. The smaller Caribbean countries all represent significant markets, that are increasing each year.

Today, modern ship captains still sail from around the world to Florida's deep water seaports, which are among the most sophisticated and cost effective in the world. With year-round good weather, and an extensive network of railroads and highways, Florida's ports handle every shipping need: containers, dry or wet bulk cargos, heavy lift machinery, refrigerated goods, barge loads, and industrial materials. Florida is also the world's largest port for automobiles. Every year, millions of tons of general cargo—both import and export—are moved through the ports of Florida. General export cargo consists of citrus fruit, vegetables, juice products, fish, lumber, paper products, clay, insecticides, poultry, sand, scrap metal, and tallow. Imported are steel, lumber, motor vehicles, machinery, marble, meat, newsprint, olives, alcoholic beverages, and bananas, as well as a host of other products. Most of Florida's massive tonnage, however, is bulk cargo. For instance, phosphate and related fertilizers constitute the most important Florida export. Inbound bulk commodities are petroleum, aragonite, coal, gypsum, calcium nitrate, and cement. By far, petroleum products account for the largest proportion of these Florida imports.

Port of Tampa, 1952
Phosphate loading elevator of the Atlantic Coast Line railroad.

Modern Ports

Pensacola

This well-protected, deep-water harbor was used by the Spanish at least as far back as 1559. It has been important to the maritime trade in the Gulf of Mexico through the centuries. Major cargo includes bagged agricultural products, chemicals, liquid petroleum, general dry bulk cargo, and forest products.

Jacksonville

This port was established in the early 19th century when Florida was a territory of the United States. Its fortunes have ebbed and flowed. It is now one of the principal ports in the world for the importation of motor vehicles. Jacksonville is Florida's largest container port, and it is a major importer of coffee. Approximately 16 million tons of cargo are handled annually. Major exports consist of paper products, fiberboard, wood pulp, and iron and steel products.

Tampa

Established as a port in the early 19th century, Tampa is Florida's largest port and ranks eighth in tonnage in the United States due to its phosphate shipments and receipt of petroleum products. It has the largest dockside cold storage in the nation. Vast amounts of fresh citrus are exported, and motor vehicles are the principal import. Sulphur, potash, and ammonia are imported as raw materials, and combined with phosphate in the manufacture of chemical fertilizer. The port has several cruise ships, and operates scheduled cargo service to Central and South America and the Caribbean, as well as service to North America, Europe, and Asia.

Canaveral

This small and efficient port got its start in 1939. It is important as a citrus shipping point and a frozen meats reception point. Cement, petroleum and scrap are also handled. The port also has cruise terminals for passenger ships

Pensacola

Jacksonville

Canaveral

Tampa

Port Manatee

Palm Beach

Port Everglades

Miami

Ports

Intracoastal Waterway and Navigable Rivers

Palm Beach

This small, compact port dates its beginning from 1915. It handles general cargo in bulk and in containers. Cargos include cement, sugar, fuel oil, and molasses. It enjoys a large trade with the Bahama Islands.

Port Manatee

Port Manatee on Tampa Bay started operation in 1971. Since that time, it has grown tremendously. It handles phosphate, fertilizers, cement, petroleum, and a small amount of general cargo, such as plywood and steel. New commodities include bananas, plantains, yams, fungicides, bagged starch, and steel cable.

Port Everglades

Established in 1927 between Fort Lauderdale and Hollywood, it is Florida's deepest natural port. The principal import is petroleum, and other commodities include steel, cement, lumber, newsprint, citrus, and containerized general cargo. Port Everglades is world famous as a port of call and departure for cruise ships; a quarter of a million passengers embark there every year.

Miami

The Port of Miami is the southernmost seaport in the continental United States and the transshipment hub of the Americas. More sailings to Central and South America and the Caribbean originate from Miami than any other port in the world. The city has been a port since the late 19th century, but its real prominence began in 1960 when several spoil islands in Biscayne Bay were consolidated to create the modern port. It has grown tremendously since that time, handling up to two million tons of general cargo annually. Miami is also known as the "Cruise Capital of the World," serving over a million passengers each year.

Navigation and Ship Types

Navigational Tools

Navigation is a matter of knowing where in the world you are compared to where in the world you want to go. Navigational tools have increased in accuracy and in ease of use throughout history, producing better charts and navigation instructions, better knowledge of actual and planned courses, and an increased chance of arriving safely at the intended destination. During the voyages of exploration and discovery, errors in position finding were on the order of tens of miles or more. Modern, satellite-based systems can be accurate to within inches.

Lead and Line

The sounding lead consists of a hemp line, marked at intervals for depth, to which is attached a lead weight. A hollow in the bottom of the weight can be "armed" with tallow to catch a sample of the seabottom sediments, telling the leadsman the type of bottom he is finding in addition to the depth. Early Spanish sailing directions for the Gulf of Mexico often included descriptions of bottom sediments and depths encountered on the approach to Florida.

Sand Glass

Before the development of reliable shipboard clocks, the sand glass was the only means of measuring the passage of time at sea, a task which was essential for navigational reckoning. Sand from the upper globe ran down into the lower; the glass was then inverted and the process repeated in the same interval of time. Half-hour sand glasses were used by most ships; a bell was rung at each interval, and at eight bells (four hours) the ship's watch changed.

Compass

Still the principal instrument for navigation, the magnetic compass was in use at sea as early as the 12th century. A magnetized needle was attached to a circular card, on which the points of the compass were painted. The card pivoted inside a bowl, which protected the card. Until magnetic deviation of the earth and local attraction by iron ship fittings were recognized, the magnetic compass was an imperfect instrument.

Astrolabe

Used at sea to measure the altitude of the sun or a star, the astrolabe consisted of an alidade, or sighting rule, which pivoted in the center of a ring of brass inscribed with degrees of arc. The astrolabe was suspended vertically by the thumb, while the alidade was turned about its axis so that the sun or star could be sighted along it. The altitude was read from the ring. This instrument was the forerunner of today's sextant.

Backstaff

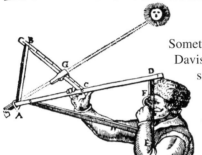

Sometimes called the Davis quadrant, this simple instrument measured the altitude of the sun without sighting it directly. With his back to the sun, the observer viewed the horizon through an eye slit, and aligned it with the forward end of a graduated staff, moving a curved arc back and forth until its shadow coincided with the horizon. The sum of the two angles indicated on the staff and arc was the sun's altitude.

Recording Log

The name "log" comes from a piece of wood thrown overboard at the bow of a ship and timed as it passed to the stern to estimate the ship's speed. This inaccurate system was eventually replaced by a mechanical or recording log, consisting of a rotator on a long line, which was attached at the stern to a register calibrated to record distance on a series of dials. The distance recorded in one-hour intervals gave the speed of the ship through the water.

LORAN

Developed during World War II, LOng RAnge Navigation (LORAN) is a radio navigational system which uses pulsed transmissions from master to slave stations. Measurement of the time interval between the arrival of the radio transmissions at the ship gives a position line; a second reading from another pair of stations produces another position line, allowing a navigational fix to be obtained.

Satellite Positioning System

The latest and most accurate instruments are those used in a global positioning system (GPS), which is a space-based radio navigational network of satellites circling the globe every 12 hours beaming continuous navigational signals to Earth. A navigator with a GPS receiver need only push a few buttons to automatically select the most favorably located satellites, lock onto their signals, and compute the user's position, speed, and time.

Ship Types

Caravel

The Spanish caravel was a familiar vessel type during the Age of Discovery. Perhaps the most famous caravel, *Niña*, was Columbus' favorite ship. Built for seaworthiness rather than cargo capacity, the caravel was adapted from fishing vessels by the Portuguese, who used such ships to explore the coast of Africa. A combination of fore-and-aft lateen sails, a narrow and shallow hull, and an axial stern rudder produced the most efficient sailing machine of its time.

Two of Columbus's former crew members, Juan Ponce de León and Antón de Alaminos, sighted the coast of Florida in 1513 from the caravel *Santiago*, flagship of a small fleet of three vessels. Sailing southward along the Atlantic coast, through the Keys, and up the Gulf coast, Ponce was not sure whether he had discovered a large island or not; but pilot Alaminos had noted a phenomenon that would impact all subsequent navigation in the region—the Gulf Stream, a natural current that would propel future Spanish shipping homeward from the Caribbean. In 1517, Alaminos returned to the coast of Florida as pilot in a small fleet of caravels commanded by Francisco Hernández de Córdoba. Caravels supported the expedition of Hernando de Soto to Florida in 1539, and were among the ill-fated fleet of Tristán de Luna y Arellano during the first Spanish attempt to colonize Florida in 1559.

Galleon

The galleon was associated with the early Spanish settlements of Florida. Armed freighters of the maritime lifeline between Spain and her colonies, galleons were developed in response to a need for transatlantic speed and security. Galleons combined the cargo capacity of heavy, round ships and the swift waterlines of oared galleys with the sail patterns and rigging of oceanic caravels to become among the most advanced sailing ships of their day. By the middle of the 16th century, galleons averaged between 300 and 600 tons; later in the century, they grew to 1200 tons. Even under the best conditions, these "castles of the sea" could not average more than four or five knots in favorable winds.

Three major fleet disasters in the years 1622, 1715, and 1733 wrecked scores of Spanish galleons along the Florida coast. *Urca de Lima*, one of the ships driven ashore near modern-day Ft. Pierce by a hurricane in 1715, has been designated as a state Underwater Archaeological Preserve. *San Pedro*, a victim of the 1733 hurricane that wrecked over 20 ships along the Florida reef, is the site of another Preserve near Islamorada. Both shipwrecks are visited annually by hundreds of snorkelers and divers.

Frigate

Frigates were employed by most European navies in the 18th century. They were strong, swift vessels built for all-weather seaworthiness and were used in convoy and privateering service. Well armed for their size, frigates supported Spanish and English occupations of East and West Florida during the European contest for colonial control of North America and the Caribbean. Small frigates stationed at St. Augustine and Pensacola carried 18 to 20 guns and patrolled Florida's coasts to guard against enemy corsairs. One such vessel was HMS *Mentor*, an American-built privateer captured by the British and sent to Pensacola in 1780 to protect the West Florida colony against Spanish forces in New Orleans. The small frigate of 220 tons carried eighteen 12-pound and six 4-pound guns, and was the best armed vessel in the port when the Spanish fleet attacked Pensacola in 1781. To bolster the defenses of the British fort, her captain removed the ship's crew and guns, ordering the *Mentor* up a shallow river to avoid its capture. When a sudden squall capsized the frigate, it was set on fire and abandoned. The city surrendered to the Spaniards, and in 1783 the British rule of Florida ended.

Schooner

Schooners were fore-and-aft rigged sailing ships used for coastal trade and in the fishing industry. Usually two-masted, schooners required smaller crews and sailed faster than square-rigged ships, but could carry less cargo. The schooner was a familiar craft in Florida's waters from colonial times until the early 20th century. Employed by merchants to ship cotton, lumber and bricks, by fishermen to catch schools of red snapper, by smugglers and blockade runners to carry clandestine cargos, and by wreckers to salvage goods from grounded vessels, schooners were also used by the U.S. Navy to suppress pirates and slave traders.

One such schooner, USS *Alligator*, a 175-ton warship, was outfitted at Boston in 1821 with 10 six-pound and 2 eight-pound guns. In that same year, the United States acquired Florida from Spain, and the federal government sent *Alligator* to hunt pirates off the southern coast of the new territory. In November, 1822, the naval schooner seized a pirate ship off Cuba; during the fight the commander of the American vessel was killed. Ten days later, the *Alligator* ran aground on the Florida Reef near Indian Key. Her crew was forced to abandon the schooner, and they blew up the ship to keep it out of pirate hands. Later, this section of reef was officially named for the schooner. Today the ship's remains, covered with coral, lie a stone's throw from Alligator Reef Lighthouse, which was built 51 years after the disaster.

Steamboat

In the early 1800s, as steam began to be used for watercraft propulsion, steamboats gradually appeared along Florida's coasts and navigable rivers. Large coastal steamers connected Florida with Georgia, South Carolina, and the Gulf of Mexico. Smaller river steamers carried passengers, freight, and mail to growing inland settlements. The St. Johns River was a major artery for steam traffic in East Florida. In the west, the Apalachicola and Suwannee Rivers were navigated by boats with shallow drafts.

Propelled by paddlewheels mounted on the side or in the stern, steamboats had either one or two decks and engines mounted aft of midships. The age of steamboating in Florida lasted almost a hundred years until the advent of railroads and larger steamships reduced the role of the steamboat to one of catering to visitors and vacation travelers. A good example of Florida's golden age of steam is the *City of Hawkinsville*, a well-preserved steamboat lying at the bottom of the Suwannee River near Old Town. *Hawkinsville* was 141 feet long, with two decks and two recirculating steam engines that powered a stern paddlewheel. Abandoned by her captain in the 1920s, the sunken boat was nominated by local divers to become a state Underwater Archaeological Preserve and was designated in 1991.

Steamship

Capable of arriving on schedule despite head winds, rough weather, or opposing tides, the steamship brought order and dependability to Florida's 19th-century waterborne commerce. Regular scheduled voyages and increased cargo capacity opened a new era in Florida's trade with North and South America and Europe; more voyages meant more cargo and more profit, as merchant shipping, together with railroads, opened up new areas of Florida's coastline to trade and industry. Regular steamship packet service, carrying mail, passengers, and cargo on a set schedule, was inaugurated at Jacksonville, linking Florida with the wider world. In steamships, paddle wheels were gradually replaced by propellors. Increasing use of iron and steel in shipbuilding allowed larger vessels to be built to carry greater amounts of cargo to and from Florida's major seaports, which began to be improved by dredging and construction of wharves and piers. A good example of a single screw steamship is the SS *Copenhagen*, which wrecked off Pompano Beach in 1900.

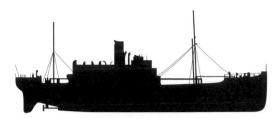

Freighter

At the turn of the century, steam turbines began to replace simple and compound steam engines on merchant vessels. Efficiency was further increased as a shift from coal to oil boosted the cruising range of cargo carriers. Freighters using this technology differed only in dimensions and refinements from today's cargo ships. The bow and stern of the freighter's steel hull were raised high above the water to keep waves from breaking on deck. A central deckhouse contained the crew's quarters, and the navigation bridge was above the engine spaces. Watertight holds were served by cargo booms on fore and aft masts, which lifted goods in and out of hatches with the help of steam winches. Today, freighters of all sizes, flags, and ages are to be found trading in Florida's major and minor seaports. They carry almost every kind of cargo imaginable, and represent the largest class of merchant ships in the water. The most famous freighter in Florida is the *Mercedes I*, which was thrown high and dry by a storm onto the seawall of a wealthy Palm Beach resident in 1984. Later made an artificial reef, the *Mercedes* is a popular diving destination.

Container Ship

As the first new type of oceangoing merchant vessel since the introduction of the tanker, the container ship has revolutionized the handling of Florida's seaborne cargo, resulting in great savings in transportation costs. With no interior decks, and the engine room located in the stern, a container ship's hull is simply an enormous warehouse, divided into vertical racks which hold aluminum containers full of cargo. Containers are loaded below decks by special overhead cranes, or sometimes by hauling them up ramps through the bow of the ship, which is fashioned with giant doors that open onto the dock. Often, containers are carried on the open decks of transport vessels, their contents already protected from the weather. The container system allows goods to be packed in a standardized receptacle at the point of origin and delivered to their destination with no handling of the contents along the way. Containers are readily transferred between carriers; they are made to fit on a standard truck trailer and on special railroad flatcars for transportation inland.

Aircraft Carrier

The aircraft carrier was the first new type of warship invented in this century; its introduction at sea revolutionized naval combat. With squadrons of fighters, bombers, and reconnaissance aircraft on board, a carrier is a mobile air base which can operate in all oceans with great speed and power.

Florida played a key role in the development of the aircraft carrier. The Navy's first carrier, USS *Langley*, conducted experimental operations at the Pensacola Naval Air Station between 1923 and 1924. The second carrier, USS *Saratoga*, was also sent to Pensacola to conduct secret experiments in 1928. By 1930, aircraft carriers had become an active part of American naval forces.

Both World War II and the Korean War demonstrated the strategic value of the aircraft carrier. In the

early 1950s, the Navy began to build a fleet of "super carriers" that included USS *Forrestal* (CV-59) as a prototype. A new USS *Saratoga* (CV-60), commissioned in 1956, began her career in Florida, homeported

Battleship

The oldest surviving American battleship, USS *Massachusetts* (BB-2), has spent 70 of its 100 years submerged under Florida's water. Commissioned in 1896, the warship belonged to the Indiana class of three coastal battleships built before the Spanish-American War. Florida was a major staging area for that war. The largest military expedition ever to leave the United States assembled in Tampa to embark on transports for Cuba. The small naval station at Key West rapidly became the major naval base of the war. *Indiana* led the convoy from Florida to Cuba; her sister ship, *Oregon,* rounded the tip of South America to reach Key West and joined the Cuba blockade. *Massachusetts* joined the Navy's "Flying Squadron" in Key West to converge on the Spanish fleet at Santiago with other battleships.

In 1921, stripped of her guns, *Massachusetts* was towed to Pensacola as a target for experimental artillery tests. Somewhat worse for wear, her remains became popular with local fishermen and divers, who in 1990 nominated the ship to become Florida's fourth Underwater Archaeological Preserve.

Cruise Ship

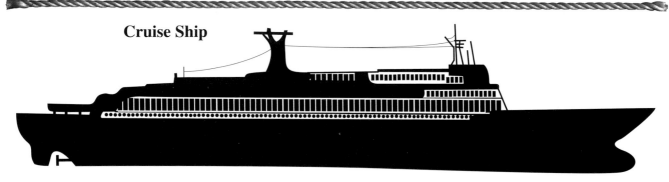

Mass air travel in the 1960s spelled the end of an era for ocean liners as a primary mode of transportation. The modern cruise industry offers seaborne vacations instead of speed and transport. Today's cruise ships carry as few as 112 passengers, and as many as 2,600. Aside from traditional shipboard facilities, such as dining rooms, lounges, theaters, and swimming pools, many liners feature full-service health spas, casinos, and conference centers. Today, over 36 modern passenger ships use Florida ports to embark on cruises that range from 3 to 98 days at sea, and from weekend Bahama visits to voyages around the globe.

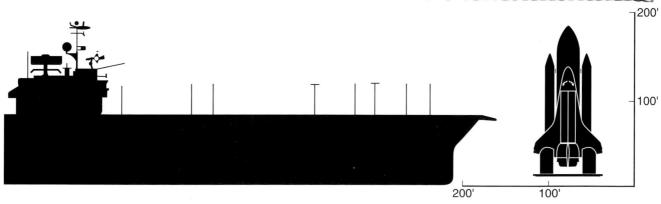

at Mayport. Decommissioned in 1995, she was replaced by the carrier *John F. Kennedy* (CV-67), which carries 80 aircraft and a crew over 5,000 officers and enlisted personnel, and has a speed of over 30 knots. Pensacola for years served as a homeport for USS *Lexington* (CV-16), on which most of today's naval aviators were trained. In 1992, *Lexington* was replaced by *Forrestal*, which was decommissioned only a year later.

Hazards and Aids to Navigation

Navigation is the art of arriving safely and on schedule at an intended destination. Our maritime navigation system is based on supplying aids where hazards are greatest.

Hurricanes

Of all the natural and cultural factors that affect maritime activities, none is more powerful than the hurricane. Even today's massive steel-hulled vessels driven by powerful engines are like toys before the winds and seas of a Category 5 hurricane. The devastating effect of a large hurricane on an entire convoy of sailing ships is graphically documented in historical accounts of the 1715 and 1733 plate fleet disasters. The modern technology of weather prediction and communication can now provide early warning and accurate tracking of hurricanes so that ships can avoid or prepare for these storms. However, as late as the beginning of the 20th century, the only warning of a potentially disastrous storm was the weather change recognizable by experienced seamen.

Florida extends into the Caribbean basin in a way which makes it particularly exposed to these storms that develop far out to sea. As they traverse the open ocean, there is little obstruction to dissipate their growing force. The Florida coast receives the full brunt of the wind, tide, and surge, driving vessels at sea or in harbor further inland. Sailing ships caught unawares on the lower east coast found their anchors of little use against the shoreward winds; often, before reaching shore, the vessels struck bottom on the rocky fringing reefs and were broken up. Even today, large vessels are driven ashore on storm surges of ten feet or more, and are left high and dry far from the shoreline.

Knowledge of the distribution of hurricanes in time and space is important in understanding their effect on maritime activities. The 20th-century data, presented at right, is assumed to be typical of earlier historical periods. It is clear that hurricanes occur only in certain months, namely June through November. Hurricanes are both most frequent and strongest in the months of September and October. As the Spanish fleets assembled in the spring in Cuba to sail in convoy to Spain, sailors became more worried as each bureaucratic delay postponed the departure date into the summer months.

Hurricanes also have a definite spatial pattern, as shown by the map of storm intensity and landfall location. The lower east coast and the Keys receive not only the greatest number of hurricanes, but also the most intense storms. The large proportion of Florida shipwrecks in this section of the state is due to a combination of factors–shipping routes that follow the Gulf Stream through the narrow Florida Channel, the existence of fringing reefs, and the distribution of hurricanes.

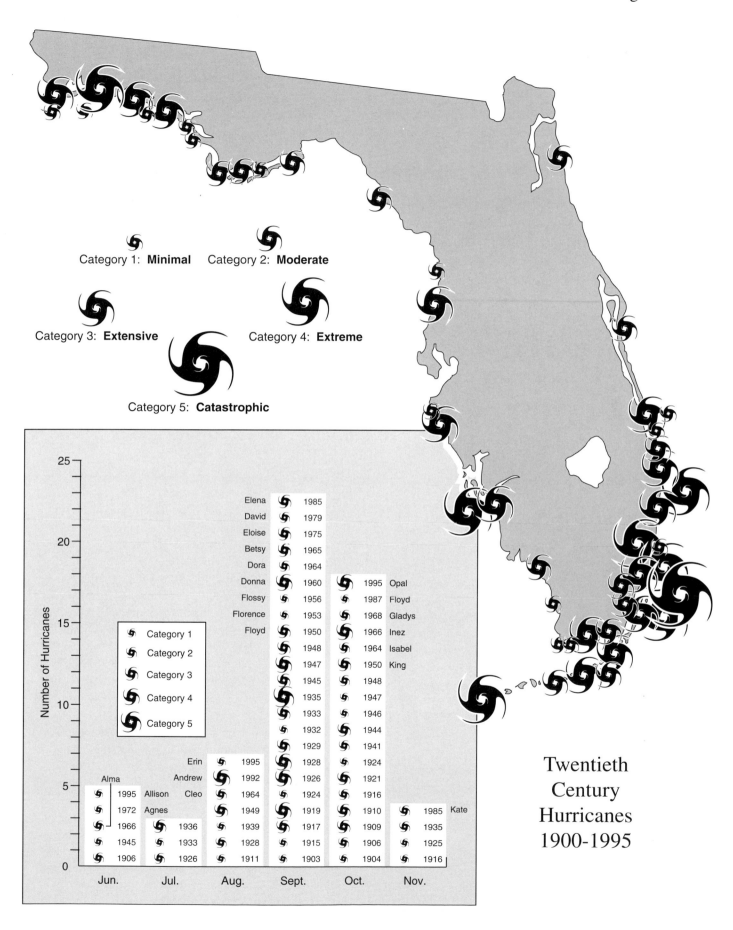

Category 1: **Minimal**   Category 2: **Moderate**

Category 3: **Extensive**   Category 4: **Extreme**

Category 5: **Catastrophic**

Twentieth
Century
Hurricanes
1900-1995

	Category 1
	Category 2
	Category 3
	Category 4
	Category 5

Number of Hurricanes

	Jun.		Jul.		Aug.		Sept.		Oct.		Nov.
Elena							1985				
David							1979				
Eloise							1975				
Betsy							1965				
Dora							1964				
Donna							1960		1995	Opal	
Flossy							1956		1987	Floyd	
Florence							1953		1968	Gladys	
Floyd							1950		1966	Inez	
							1948		1964	Isabel	
							1947		1950	King	
							1945		1948		
							1935		1947		
							1933		1946		
							1932		1944		
							1929		1941		
				Erin		1995	1928		1924		
Alma			Andrew		1992	1926		1921		
	1995	Allison	Cleo		1964	1924		1916		
	1972	Agnes			1949	1919		1910		1985	Kate
	1966		1936		1939	1917		1909		1935	
	1945		1933		1928	1915		1906		1925	
	1906		1926		1911	1903		1904		1916	

Reefs, Shoals, and Obstructions

As if strategically fashioned to trap ships, the Florida Straits are a notorious shipping passage. Bordered by hidden coral walls, subject to erratic and often violent weather conditions, and swept by the flow of the Gulf Stream, the Straits were, and still are, a major avenue to be treated with respect by mariners. On the Stream's western side, the Florida Reef is one of five major danger areas for coastal and ocean-going vessels traveling along the Atlantic coast of North America. Shallow water, shoals, and eddying currents combine to produce uniquely dangerous maritime conditions. Aside from hurricanes, annual autumn and winter storms blew sailing ships off course and onto the reef. Many wrecks occurred, and still occur, in calm weather and quiet seas because of erratic drift and the sometimes deceptive appearance of the reef in places.

Five to seven miles offshore, shoals covered with living corals run parallel to the Florida Keys. Vessels heading south traditionally have sailed with a counter-current close to the Florida Reef to avoid bucking the full force of the Gulf Stream. Only at a few points do the shoals reach the surface of the sea. These are the most dangerous points for maritime traffic: Carysfort, Alligator, and Tennessee Reefs are among the worst areas. If the weather is rough, the navigation faulty, or the ship slow to answer the helm, the coral reefs rip out another bottom. Between the outer reef and the Keys is a navigable ship channel which can be reached by numerous passages through the reef. However, this channel also is full of shoals and flats that can trap unwary navigators.

Aside from reefs and shoals, barrier islands and related landforms fringe most of Florida's coastline. Almost all of the state's sandy beaches are on coastal barriers, which act as buffers between the mainland and oceanic storms. Islands on the Atlantic coast and along the Panhandle are longer than those on the west coast. Many are unstable, shifting with tides, currents, and sea level changes. Consequently, coastal navigation near shore is hazardous due to shallow water and shifting sand bars. Between the islands are inlets, often called passes in Florida. These were, and still are, critical for navigation, since they represent the access between the sea and land. However, Florida's inlets are also unstable; some are known to have shifted hundreds of feet in a year. To maintain navigation, important inlets are routinely dredged at periodic intervals; yet they remain one of the most dangerous parts of Florida's vast maritime waterways, collecting unlucky watercraft during periods of rough weather.

The schooner *Clifford N. Carver* stranded on Tennessee Reef in 1913.

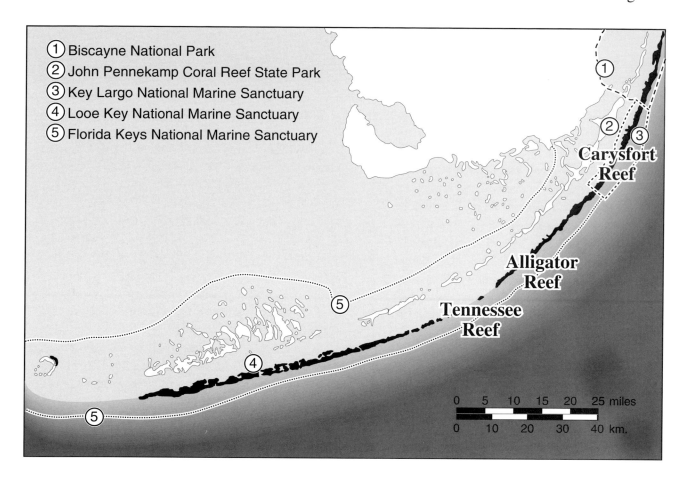

1. Biscayne National Park
2. John Pennekamp Coral Reef State Park
3. Key Largo National Marine Sanctuary
4. Looe Key National Marine Sanctuary
5. Florida Keys National Marine Sanctuary

Carysfort Reef

Alligator Reef

Tennessee Reef

0	5	10	15	20	25 miles
0	10	20	30	40 km.	

The Florida Reef

Built by lime-secreting organisms in tropical and subtropical regions where the water temperature remains above 18° C year-round, coral reefs form when larvae settle slowly on a firm substrate. Florida's reef, the largest such natural phenomena in North America, is a massive line of coral which stretches some 260 miles, from Miami to the Dry Tortugas. The main reef bank lies on the edge of the continental shelf, which steeply drops 2,400 feet into the trough of the Florida Straits through which the Gulf Stream flows. The coral rim of this great mass is not a solid wall, but forms rugged crevasses called spurs and grooves. Passages through the reef occur at intervals, but inside the outer bank are other coral structures called patch reefs, which can span several miles.

Florida's coral reef has a special value as a habitat for marine life, and is of special concern because of its vulnerability to natural and human impact. In 1960, a 75-square-mile portion of the reef off Key Largo was designated as the John Pennecamp Coral Reef State Park. Other portions of the reef at Biscayne Bay and

Dry Torgugas came to be protected as units of the National Park Service. The corals offshore Key Largo and at Looe Key were designated, in 1975 and 1981 respectively, as national marine sanctuaries administered by the National Oceanic and Atmospheric Administration (NOAA). The Florida Keys National Marine Sanctuary was created in 1990 to protect the entire reef from ship groundings, oil and gas drilling, and pollution.

Sport diving in Florida Keys National Marine Sanctuary.

Lighthouses

When the territory of Florida was annexed to the United States in 1821, there were no navigational aids to mark its dangerous, reef-strewn shores, except for an old Spanish watchtower at St. Augustine. As maritime traffic increased along the Straits of Florida and in the Gulf of Mexico, the incidence of shipwrecks and piracy also increased, prompting mariners to ask the government to address these problems. The St. Augustine watchtower was replaced by a 73-foot lighthouse in 1824, which was the first of Florida's navigational sentinels. A naval base was created at Key West to suppress piracy, and Congress appropriated funds for the Lighthouse Service to construct an 85-foot lighthouse there, a 60-foot light on nearby Sand Key, and a 75-foot tower on Garden Key in the Dry Tortugas. Dangerous Carysfort Reef off Key Largo was given a lightship because it seemed impossible at the time to build a lighthouse on the reef itself. A 65-foot tower was erected on Cape Florida at the southeastern tip of Key Biscayne, and another lighthouse was built at Pensacola to serve its proposed naval yard. Between 1830 and 1850, lights were erected along much of Florida's east and west coasts to mark islands, inlets, and river mouths for shipping. These included towers at Amelia Island, St. Johns River, Ponce de Leon Inlet, Cape Canaveral, and in the Gulf of Mexico at Egmont Key, St. Marks, Dog Island, Cape St. George, Cape San Blas, and St. Joseph Bay.

Despite the construction of lighthouses on land, the treacherous reefs of the Florida Keys remained unmarked except for the Carysfort Lightship, and a lightship stationed at Sand Key after its tower was demolished in a hurricane. Masonry towers built on sand simply could not withstand waves and storm tides, and were not suitable for the shallow reefs and bars of Florida. The newly created Lighthouse Board decided to try a revolutionary piling design developed in the 1830s by an English engineer. Wrought iron piles, screwed into the soft seabed, supported a platform for the light, and offered little resistance to winds and waves. Construction of screw-pile lighthouses in Florida began at Carysfort Reef, where the new design replaced the lightship in 1852. Soon, pile lighthouses illuminated the Florida Reef from Fowey Rocks to Sand Key, representing a series of unprecedented engineering

accomplishments. These Reef Lights still stand and are in use today, although electric timers and photosensitive cells have eliminated the need for lightkeepers.

Today, some thirty lighthouses guide mariners around the coast of Florida, from St. Marys River to the

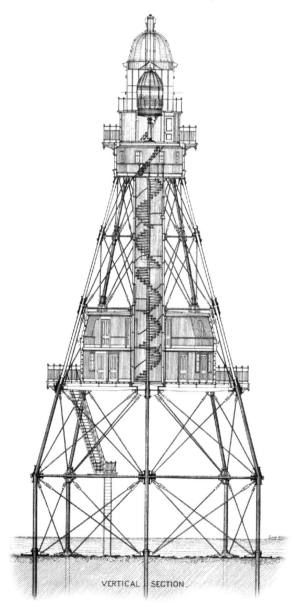

VERTICAL SECTION.

American Shoal Lighthouse
The last lighthouse to be built on the dangerous reefs of the Florida Keys, American Shoal light was completed in 1880 at a cost of $125,000. Prefabricated parts were assembled beforehand at a northern foundry to assure a perfect fit prior to shipping them to Key West. A special boat was built to carry the lighthouse parts to the construction site. The light is 109 feet above the water, and is visible from 13 miles away on a clear night.

Dry Tortugas, then north to Pensacola Bay. Administration of these aids to navigation has changed hands over the years, from the Lighthouse Board to the Bureau of Lighthouses to the United States Coast Guard. Many have been incorporated into parks, wildlife refuges, and recreational areas, and nearly all have been placed on the National Register of Historic Places. With a distinctive color for daytime recognition and unique light sequence for nocturnal identification, each is a functional relic of maritime Florida.

Cape Canaveral Lighthouse
Perched near the launchpads of spacecraft, Cape Canaveral Light was completed after the Civil War and given a lens that mariners could see 18 miles offshore. When the sea encroached on its location, the tower was rebuilt in 1894 on its present site, a mile farther inland. Today, the lighthouse still serves shipping, including Polaris submarines that use nearby Port Canaveral.

Pensacola

St. Joseph Bay

Cape San Blas

Cape St. George

St. Marks

Crooked River

Seahorse Key

Anclote Key

Egmont Key

Gasparilla Island

Boca Grande

Sanibel Island

Amelia Island

Mayport

St. Johns River

St. Augustine

Ponce de Leon Inlet

Cape Canaveral

Jupiter Inlet

Hillsboro Inlet

Cape Florida

Fowey Rocks

Carysfort Reef

Fort Jefferson

Key West

Loggerhead Key

Sand Key

American Shoal

Sombrero Key

Alligator Reef

Ship Losses and Shipwrecks

Fleet Disasters

1622- On September 4, 1622, a fleet of 28 ships sailed out of Havana harbor, bound for Spain with a wealth of precious cargo loaded at ports in South and Central America. The fleet consisted of eight large galleons, escorted by eleven guard ships and three small scout vessels. Their cargos included gold and silver specie and bullion, copper ore, tobacco, indigo, cochineal, and rosewood, as well as commercial revenues belonging to King Philip IV. The fleet did not depart until well into the hurricane season, due to delays in port. As the ships approached the Florida Keys, an enormous hurricane struck and scattered the fleet. Eight ships were lost with hundreds of seamen and passengers; the remaining vessels survived the storm and eventually made their way back to Havana.

Spanish salvors were immediately sent to the disaster area from Cuba and managed to recover parts of the cargos of two large galleon wrecks. A third, *Nuestra Señora de Atocha*, was initially found intact in deep water, but after being dispersed by a later storm, she could not be relocated. The *Atocha* remained lost until 1985, when after years of searching, modern treasure hunters found the main portion of the wreckage, which had been scattered over twelve miles of shifting sands.

1715- Eleven ships of a combined convoy from Colombia and Mexico embarked from Havana on July 24, 1715 to return to Spain. Aside from New World exports and goods from the Orient, the ships carried registered cargos of gold and silver amounting to almost seven million pieces-of-eight, representing a four-year accumulation of coins and bullion from American mints. An additional fortune in contraband bullion was probably also on board.

On July 31, borne northward through the Florida Straits by the Gulf Stream, the ships were struck by a hurricane and driven one after another onto the coastal shoals and reefs between modern-day Ft. Pierce and Sebastian Inlet. There was a salvage effort by the Spanish, but much of the ships' cargos remained strewn beneath surf and sand. In the 1940s and 50s, beachcombers along Florida's east coast began to find encrusted coins, and traced their source offshore. By 1960, the discovery of several 1715 wrecksites and associated survivors' camps on shore had started a modern gold rush that gave the name Treasure Coast to this region. The buried remains of ships' cargos have been legally and illegally salvaged by treasure hunters over the ensuing years.

1733- On the unlucky Friday of July 13, 1733, another fleet embarked from Havana on its return voyage to Spain. Four armed galleons escorted eighteen merchant ships and several smaller vessels toward the Florida Keys. The next day, the convoy's commander, sensing an approaching hurricane, ordered the ships to turn back. Already it was too late. By nightfall, most of the ships had been scattered 80 miles up and down the Keys; sunk and swamped, their survivors gathered in small groups throughout the low islands. Only a single ship returned safely to Havana to report the disastrous news. Nine salvage vessels loaded with food and supplies, divers, soldiers, and salvage gear immediately sailed northward.

Salvors marked the location of each wreck on a map, and continued their work for years; vessels that could not be refloated were burned to the waterline for access by divers and to conceal them from freebooters. A calculation of salvaged materials showed that more gold and silver had been recovered than had been listed on the ships' manifests, a result of inevitable contraband. In recent decades, the wrecks of the 1733 fleet have been relocated by divers, explored by treasure hunters, and are finally being recorded by archaeologists for their historical and recreational value.

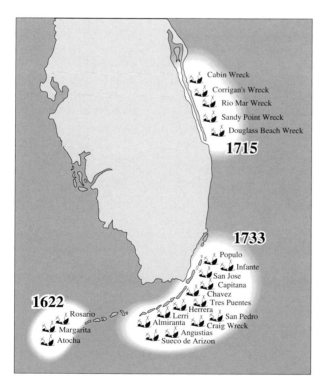

From soon after Columbus' landfall to the middle of the 18th century, Spanish fleets carried the enormous wealth of the Americas across the Atlantic to European ports. Among the most famous shipwrecks in Florida waters are the three fleets destroyed by hurricanes in 1622, 1715, and 1733. Their general locations are shown above.

Stages of a Shipwreck

The main structure of the ship, together with its keel and ballast, sinks to the sea bed. Depending on the circumstances of its sinking, many materials and contents may already have been swept away by pounding waves and underwater currents. Many buoyant objects float away.

Attempts at salvage, contemporary or later, may remove armaments, timber, cargo, and other materials from the wreck site. Chemical and biological agents in the water begin to degrade and destroy the ship's hull and many of the objects scattered around the wreck.

The turbulence of waves and currents, the shifting of loose seabed material, and the force of gravity act together to bury the remains of the ship. Exposed materials continue to erode, but buried portions, protected from further degradation by layers of silt and mud, will last almost indefinitely.

A historic wrecksite becomes a priceless historical resource, and a thriving artificial reef. Although these sites have often been dug up by treasure hunters, historic wrecks are protected by laws to ensure the conservation of our maritime heritage for future generations.

Shipwrecks

Shipwrecks in Florida are known from two sources of information. They are reported in historical documents such as government records, newspaper accounts, and insurance claims; and they are found on the seabed. Many of the ships known from records to have been lost have never been located, and many of the ships found on the seabed have never been identified as to name. Few shipwrecks found on the seabed have been thoroughly studied and documented to reveal their age, type, and nationality. Finally, some shipwreck sites are badly broken up and dispersed, and are difficult to understand even when they are carefully studied.

With these limitations it should be clear that an analysis of shipwrecks in time and space will reveal only general patterns of distribution. The graph below shows for each year between 1500 and 1950 the number of shipwrecks recorded for Florida. Locations for many of these, particularly in the early centuries, are extremely vague. There is no guarantee that such wrecks are even within the state's territorial limits. The recognized historical periods of Florida are indicated at the bottom of the chart and the periods of war are indicated on the chart. Finally, the occurrence of major hurricanes that caused reported ship losses is shown by symbol.

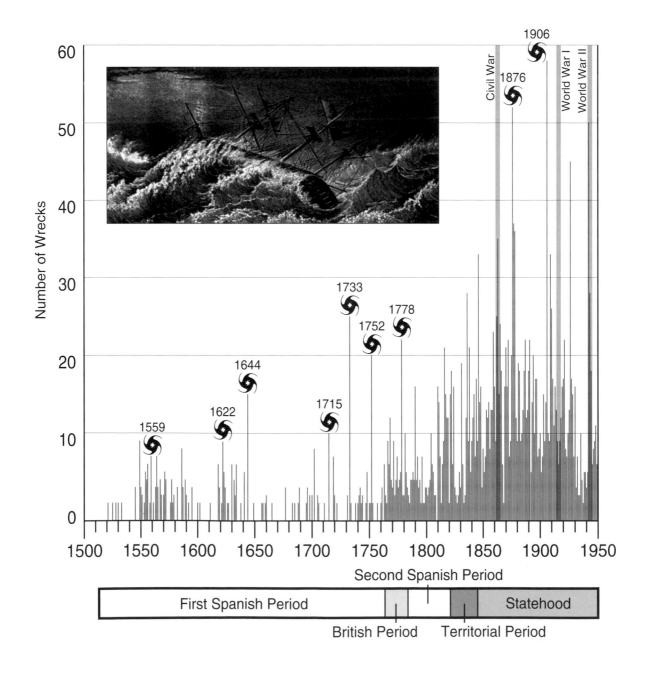

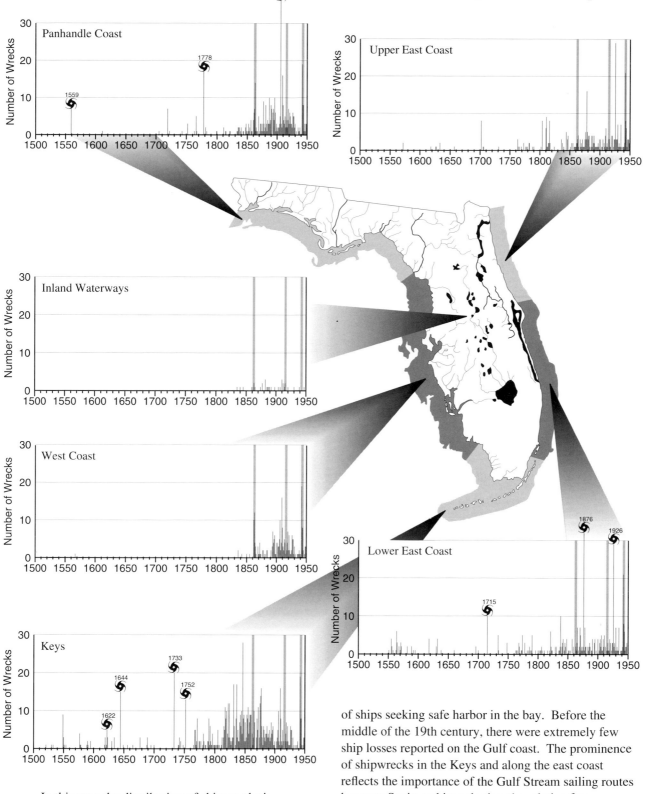

In this map the distribution of shipwrecks is further broken down into regions of Florida to show how ship losses varied geographically over time. The separate graphs are for five different stretches of the Florida coast and for all inland waterways. The importance of hurricanes in the Keys and lower east coast is apparent; the severe 1906 hurricane in Pensacola destroyed scores of ships seeking safe harbor in the bay. Before the middle of the 19th century, there were extremely few ship losses reported on the Gulf coast. The prominence of shipwrecks in the Keys and along the east coast reflects the importance of the Gulf Stream sailing routes between Spain and its colonies, the relative frequency and severity of hurricanes in this portion of the state, and the hazardous reefs in the Keys and along the lower east coast. Inland waterway losses are few in number and occur mainly in the first century of statehood, with the opening of Florida's interior to settlement and the development of steamboats.

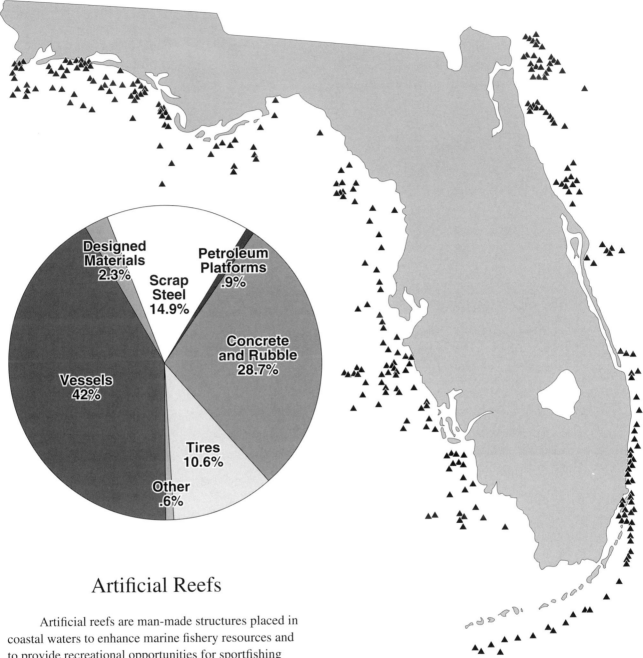

Artificial Reefs

Artificial reefs are man-made structures placed in coastal waters to enhance marine fishery resources and to provide recreational opportunities for sportfishing and diving. Local civic groups and government organizations have been involved in the construction of artificial reefs for several decades, and today artificial reefs are recognized as an important component of coastal resource management.

Florida leads the United States in the number of active permitted artificial reefs. Since 1918, when the first reef application was filed, over 400 artificial reefs have been permitted. Many of the early reefs have become buried or scattered in storms, but over 330 documented reefs remain along Florida's coastline. Accidental sinkings and deliberate dumping have added a number of "midnight reefs" (those without permits).

Early artificial reefs were built primarily of used automobile tires and other inexpensive and plentiful materials, such as surplus household appliances and used plumbing fixtures. However, these materials suffered from dispersal, deterioration, and corrosion over the years, losing their effectiveness as havens for fish. Recently, more stable reef-building materials, such as cast concrete and scrap steel, bridge rubble, large storage tanks, barges, and decommissioned ships, have been used throughout Florida. Several of the larger reefs have been constructed from Liberty ships, Coast Guard cutters, and oil drilling platforms.

Sources and Further Reading

Physical Environment:
Bathymetry and Shoreline

Sources
Fernald, Edward A., ed. 1992, *Atlas of Florida*, University Press of Florida, Gainesville.

Further reading
Cooke, C. Wythe, 1945, *The Geology of Florida.* Geological Bulletin No. 29, Florida Geological Survey, Tallahassee.

Galtsoff, Paul S., coordinator, 1954, *Gulf of Mexico, Its Origin, Waters, and Marine Life.* Fishery Bulletin of the Fish and Wildlife Service, Volume 55, United States Government Printing Office, Washington, D.C.

Hoffmeister, John Edward,1974, *Land From the Sea, The Geologic Story of South Florida.* University of Miami Press, Coral Gables, FL.

Puri, Harban S. and Robert O. Vernon, 1964, *Summary of the Geology of Florida and a Guidebook to the Classic Exposures.* Special Publication No. 5. Florida Geological Survey, Tallahassee.

State University System of Florida, Institute of Oceanography, coordinator, 1973, *A Summary of Knowledge of the Eastern Gulf of Mexico,* Tallahassee.

Winds and Currents

Sources
Fernald (1992).

National Oceanic and Atmospheric Administration, 1985, *Gulf of Mexico Coastal and Ocean Zones Strategic Assessment: Data Atlas.* U.S. Department of Commerce, Washington, D.C.

U.S. Department of the Interior, Geological Survey, 1970, *The National Atlas of the United States of America.* USGPO, Washington, D.C.

Further reading
State University System of Florida, Institute of Oceanography (1973).

Winsberg, Morton D., 1990, *Florida Weather.* University of Central Florida Press, Orlando, FL.

Growth of Maritime Florida
Native Florida

Sources
Fernald (1992).

Milanich, Jerald T. and Charles H. Fairbanks, 1980, *Florida Archaeology.* Academic Press, New York.

Purdy, Barbara, 1991, *The Art and Archaeology of Florida's Wetlands.* CRC Press, Boca Raton, FL.

Further reading
Swanton, John R., 1979, *The Indians of the Southeastern United States.* Smithsonian Institution Press, Washington, D.C. Reprint of *Bureau of American Ethnology Bulletin* 137.

Toole, Gregory, et al., 1986, "Bibliography of Florida Archaeology Through 1980." *Florida Archaeology* No. 1, pp. 1-145, Florida Bureau of Archaeological Research, Tallahassee, FL.

European Exploration and Settlement

Sources
Crosby, Alfred T., 1986, *Ecological Imperialism, The Biological Expansion of Europe, 900-1900.* Cambridge University Press, New York.

Lorant, Stefan, 1965, *The New World, The First Pictures of America.* Revised edition edited and annotated by Stefan Lorant. Duell, Sloan and Pearce, New York.

Tebeau, Charlton, 1980, *A History of Florida.* Seventh printing, revised. University of Miami Press, Coral Gables.

Further reading
Cumming, W.P., R.A. Skelton and D.B. Quinn, 1972, *The Discovery of North America.* American Heritage Press, New York.

Milanich, Jerald T. and Susan Milbrath, 1989, *First Encounters, Spanish Explorations in the Caribbean and the United States, 1492-1570.* University of Florida Press, Gainesville.

Morison, Samuel Eliot, 1974, *The European Discovery of America: The Southern Voyages, A.D. 1492-1616.* Oxford University Press, New York.

Sauer, Carl Ortwin, 1971, *Sixteenth Century North America, The Land and the People as Seen by the Europeans.* University of California Press, Berkeley.

TePaske, John Jay, 1964, *The Governorship of Spanish Florida 1700-1763.* Duke University Press, Durham, NC.

Colonial Trade

Sources
O'Connor, Thomas J., 1980, "The History of Maritime Trade in Florida," in *Florida's Maritime Heritage.* Barbara Purdy (ed.), Florida State Museum, Gainesville, pp. 29-32.

Mowat, Charles L., 1943, *East Florida as A British Province, 1763-1784.* University of California Press, Berkeley. A facsimile reproduction of the 1943 edition with an editorial preface by Rembert W. Patrick, 1964. University of Florida Press, Gainesville.

Tebeau (1980).

Further reading
Bartram, William, 1791, *Travels through North & South Carolina, Georgia, East & West Florida.* James & Johnson, Philadelphia. 1791 edition edited and with notes by Mark van Doren, 1955, Dover reprint of Macy-Masius 1928 edition, New York.

Forbes, James Grant, 1821, *Sketches, Historical and Topographicall, of the Floridas; More Particularly of East Florida.* A facsimile reproduction of the 1821 edition with an introduction by James W. Covington, 1964. University of Florida Press, Gainesville.

Mahon, John K., 1967, *History of the Second Seminole War, 1835-1842.* University of Florida Press, Gainesville.

Vignoles, Charles, 1823, *Observations upon The Floridas.* A facsimile reproduction of the 1823 New York edition, edited with an introduction and index by John Hebron Moore, 1977. University Presses of Florida, Gainesville.

Expansion of Maritime Commerce

Sources
O'Connor (1980).

Tebeau (1980).

Thurston, William N., 1972, A Study of Maritime Activity in Florida in the Nineteenth Century, Ph.D. dissertation, Florida State University, Tallahassee.

Further reading
Davis, William Watson, 1913, *The Civil War and Reconstruction in Florida.* Columbia University Press, New York.

Lanier, Sidney, 1875, *Florida: Its Scenery, Climate and History.* A facsimile reproduction of the 1875 edition with introduction and index by Jerrell H. Shofner, 1973. University of Florida Press, Gainesville.

Martin, Sidney Walter, 1949, *Florida's Flagler.* University of Georgia Press, Athens.

Modern Maritime Industry

Sources
Fernald (1992).

O'Connor (1980).

Tebeau (1980).

Further reading
Derr, Mark, 1989, *Some Kind of Paradise, A Chronicle of Man and the Land in Florida.* William Morrow and Company, Inc., New York.

Federal Writers' Project, Works Progress Administration, 1939, *Florida, A Guide to the Southernmost State.* Oxford University Press, New York.

Jahoda, Gloria, 1967, *The Other Florida.* Scribner's, New York.

Morris, Allen, editor, various years, *The Florida Handbook.* The Peninsular Publishing Company, Tallahassee.

Maritime Industries
Wrecking

Sources
Dodd, Dorothy, 1944, "The Wrecking Business on the Florida Reef," *Florida Historical Quarterly,* 22(4): 171-199.

Hammond, E. A., 1963, "Wreckers and Wrecking on the Florida Reef, 1829-1832," *Florida Historical Quarterly,* 41(1): 239-273.

Harding, George, 1911, "Wreckers of the Florida Keys," *Harper's Magazine,* July 1911, pp. 275-285.

Further reading
Shepard, Birse, 1961, *Lore of the Wreckers.* Beacon Press, Boston.

Smuggling

Sources
Greenhaw, Wayne, 1984, *Flying High. Inside Big-Time Drug Smuggling.* Dodd, Mead and Company, Inc., New York.

Waters, Harold, 1971, *Smugglers of Spirits.* Hastings House, New York.

Further reading
Willoughby, Malcolm Francis, 1964, *Rum War at Sea.* U.S. Government Printing Office, Washington, D.C.

Lumber

Sources
Campbell, A. Stuart, "Studies in Forestry Resources in Florida, Vol II: The Lumber Industry, Vol III: The Naval Stores Industry," Gainesville: *University of Florida Economics Series*, Vol 1, Nos. 4, (1932), 5 (1934).

Further reading
Massey, Richard W., Jr., 1960, A History of the Lumber Industry in Alabama and West Florida, 1880-1914. Ph.D. dissertation, Vanderbilt University.

Tyson, Willie Kate, 1956, History of the Utilization of the Longleaf Pine (*Pinus palustris*) in Florida From 1513 Until the Twentieth Century. Master's Thesis, University of Florida, Gainesville.

Marine Recreation

Sources
Bureau of Economic Analysis, 1992, *1991 Florida Visitor Study : Executive Summary.* Florida Department of Commerce, Tallahassee.

Commercial Fishing

Sources
Baumer, David R., 1989, Fishing Vessels of the Northern Gulf Coast Red Snapper Fishery. Master's Thesis, East Carolina University, Greenville, NC.

Cato, James and Donald Sweat, 1980, "Fishing: Florida's First Industry," in Barbara Purdy ed., *Florida Maritime Heritage.* Florida State Museum, Gainesville, pp. 32-36.

Livingston, Robert J., 1983, *Resource Atlas of the Apalachicola Estuary.* Florida Sea Grant, Tallahassee.

Lyon, Eugene, 1980, "Utilization of Marine Resources by the Keys and Coastal Indians...," in Barbara Purdy ed., *Florida Maritime Heritage.* Florida State Museum, Gainesville, pp. 10-12.

Marrinan, Rochelle A. and Elizabeth S. Wing, 1980, "Prehistoric Fishing," in Barbara Purdy ed., *Florida Maritime Heritage.* Florida State Museum, Gainesville, pp. 8-10.

Historic Trade

Sources
O'Connor (1980).

Further reading
Bennett, Charles E., 1966, "Early History of the Cross-Florida Barge Canal," *Florida Historical Quarterly* 45:132-144.

Mueller, Edward A., 1962, East Coast Florida Steamboating, 1831-1861, *Florida Historical Quarterly*, 40:241-260.

Modern Trade

Sources
Florida Department of Commerce, 1989, *Florida's Seaports.* Tallahassee.

Florida House of Representatives, Commerce Committee, 1990, *Executive Summary*, Florida International Affairs and Trade Promotion Act, Tallahassee.

O'Connor (1980).

Tyler, William G., and Charles A. Wheeler, 1978, *Florida's International Trade and Its Impact on the State Economy.* University of Florida, Department of Economics, Gainesville.

U.S. Department of Commerce, International Trade Commission, 1984, *Florida Exports.* State Export Series, Washington, D.C.

Modern Ports

Sources
Florida Department of Commerce (1989).

O'Connor (1980).

Navigation and Ship Types
Navigational Tools

Sources
Bathe, Basil W., 1978, *The Visual Encyclopedia of Nautical Terms Under Sail.* Crown Publishers, New York.

Randier, Jean, 1980, *Marine Navigational Instruments.* J. Murray, London.

Further reading
Maloney, Elbert S. (ed.), 1978, *Dutton's Navigation and Piloting.* Naval Institution Press, Annapolis, MD.

Phillips-Birt, Douglas, 1971, *A History of Seamanship.* Doubleday, New York.

Ship Types

Sources
Bathe (1978).

Dunn, Lawrence, 1973, *Merchant Ships of the World in Color: 1910-1929.* MacMillan Publishing, New York.

Schonknecht, Rolf, et. al., 1983, *Ships and Shipping of Tomorrow.* Cornell Maritime Press, Centreville, MD.

Smith, Roger C., 1986, *Early modern European ship-types 1450-1650.* The Newberry Library Slide Set No. 6, Occasional Paper No. 1, The Newberry Library, Chicago.

Smith, Roger C., "Ships in the Exploration of *La Florida*," *Gulf Coast Historical Review* 8(1): 18-29.

Smith, Roger C., 1993, *Vanguard of Empire: Ships of Exploration in the Age of Columbus.* Oxford University Press, New York.

Van Orden, M. D., 1969, *The Book of United States Navy Ships.* Dodd, Mead & Company, New York.

Further reading
Bathe (1978).

Kemp, Peter (ed.), 1980, *Encyclopedia of Ships and Seafaring.* Crown Publishers, New York:.

Landström, Bjorn, 1961, *The Ship: An Illustrated History.* Doubleday, Garden City.

Hazards and Aids to Navigation
Hurricanes

Sources
Ludlum, David C., 1963, *Early American Hurricanes: 1492-1870.* American Meteorological Society, Boston.

Millas, José Carlos, 1968, *Hurricanes of the Caribbean and Adjacent Regions, 1492-1800.* Florida Academy of the Arts and Sciences of the Americas, Miami.

Winsberg, Morton D., 1990, *Florida Weather.* University of Central Florida Press, Orlando.

Further reading
Douglas, Marjory Stoneman, 1958, *Hurricane.* Rinehart, New York.

Helm, Thomas, 1967, *Hurricanes; Weather at its Worst.* Dodd, Mead, New York.

Tannehill, Ivan Ray, 1938, *Hurricanes, their nature and history, particularly those of the West Indies and the southern coasts of the United States.* Princeton University Press, Princeton.

Reefs, Shoals, and Obstructions

Sources
Jones, Owen Arthur, 1973, *Biology and Geology of Coral Reefs.* Academic Press, New York.

Sharma, Divesh C., 1981, *Barrier Islands: Nature vs. Man: How Sanibel and Captive Fit into the Pattern.* Sanibel- Captiva Conservation Foundation, Sanibel Island, FL.

The Florida Reef

Sources
Kaplan, Eugene H., 1982, *A Field Guide to Coral Reefs of the Caribbean and Florida..* Houghton Mifflin, New York.

Further reading
Agassiz, Louis, 1880, *Report on the Florida Reefs.* Harvard Museum of Comparitive Zoology, Cambridge, MA.

Lighthouses

Sources
Dean, Love, 1982, *Reef Lights: Seaswept Lighthouses of the Florida Keys.* Historic Key West Preservation Board, Key West.

De Wire, Elinor, 1987, *Guide of Florida Lighthouses*. Pineapple Press, Englewood, FL.

Further reading
Carse, Robert, 1969, *Keepers of the Lights: A History of the American Lighthouses*. Charles Scribner's Sons, New York.

McCarthy, Kevin M., 1990, *Florida Lighthouses*. University of Florida Press, Gainesville, Fl.

Ship Losses and Shipwrecks
Fleet Disasters

Sources
Burgess, Robert F. and Carl J. Clausen, 1982, *Florida's Golden Galleons*. Florida Classics Library, Port Salerno, FL.

Smith, Roger C., 1988, "The Iberian-American Maritime Empires," in George F. Bass (ed.) *Ships and Shipwrecks in the Americas, A History Based on Underwater Archaeology*. Thames and Hudson, London.

Further reading
Marx, Robert F., 1968, *The Treasure Fleets of the Spanish Main*. World Publishing Co., Cleveland.

McCarthy, Kevin M. 1992, *Thirty Florida Shipwrecks*. Pineapple Press, Sarasota, FL.

Shipwrecks

Sources
Bureau of Archaeological Research, historic shipwreck data on file, Florida Department of State, Tallahassee.

Further reading
Marx, Robert F., 1971, *Shipwrecks of the Western Hemisphere: 1492-1825*. World Publishing Co., New York.

McCarthy, Kevin M., 1992, *Thirty Florida Shipwrecks*. Pineapple Press, Sarasota, FL.

Singer, Steven, 1992, *Florida Shipwrecks*. Pineapple Press, Sarasota.

Artificial Reefs

Sources
Andree, Scott (ed.), 1988, *Florida Artificial Reef Summit*. Proceedings of a Conference Held November 2, 1987 in Miami, Florida. Florida Sea Grant College Program, Gainesville.

Pybas, Donald W., 1991, *Atlas of Artificial Reefs in Florida, Fourth Edition*. Florida Sea Grant College Program, Gainesville.